Letts
EDUCATIONAL

Exam Practice
A LEVEL

A Level
Exam Practice

Covers AS and A2

Business Studies

Authors

Stephen Wood
David Floyd

Contents

AS and A2 exams

Different types of questions

Structured questions

In A level Business Studies exams, unit tests often use structured questions requiring both short answers and more extended answers. These questions are often in several parts, each of which may be further subdivided. They may be linked directly to data on a given context in the form of a paragraph or short article about a real or imagined business situation. This introductory data provides the major part of the information to be used, and indicates clearly what the question is about.

Structured questions are popular at AS and at A2 level. The parts to these questions become progressively more demanding as you work your way through them.

Extended answers

Business Studies questions requiring more extended answers may form part of structured questions, or may form separate questions. These may also be linked to a 'scenario' or case study, and are often used to assess your ability to communicate ideas, and to assemble a logical argument. The synoptic assessment units will require some extended answers that test your ability to integrate your understanding of various Business Studies content and themes.

The 'correct' answers to extended questions are often less well-defined than those requiring shorter answers. Examiners have a list of points for which credit is awarded up to the maximum for the question.

What examiners look for

- Examiners are obviously looking for correct points, although these may not match the wording in the examiner's marking scheme exactly.

- Your answer will score high marks if it contains accurate content and shows that you can apply, analyse and evaluate this content in the context of the question. You will not receive extra marks for writing a lot of words or through simply repeating information.

- Examiners expect you to reach a logical conclusion based on the arguments presented in your answer.

What makes an A, C and E grade candidate?

Obviously, you want to get the highest grade you possibly can. The way to do this is to make sure you have a good all-round knowledge and understanding of business studies.

- **A grade candidates** have a wide knowledge of business studies and can apply that knowledge to new situations. They are equally strong in all of the modules. A likely minimum mark for an A grade candidate is 75%.

- **C grade candidates** have a reasonable knowledge of business studies, but they are less effective when applying their knowledge to new situations. They may also have weaknesses in some of the modules. A likely minimum mark for a C grade candidate is 50%.

- **E grade candidates** have a limited knowledge of business studies, and have not learnt how to apply their ideas effectively to new situations. They find it harder to express their knowledge, and fail to give full answers. A likely minimum mark for an E grade is 40%.

Successful revision

Revision skills

- Develop a 'revision routine', eg by doing revision in the same place and about the same time each day.
- Prepare a revision plan for a topic, eg review next day, then re-read two weeks later.
- Start with a topic with which you are familiar.
- Re-read topics, to reinforce your learning.
- If you make revision notes, identify key points such as the main business theme or issue.
- Vary the style of your notes, eg by producing 'spider diagrams', patterned notes or mnemonics.
- Limit the time you spend (eg 30 to 40 minutes) before taking a break.
- Stop before you get too tired.
- Leave something easy with which to start your revision the next day.
- Don't stay up late the night before an exam trying to learn new topics. You will have forgotten much of it by the morning, and the lack of sleep may affect your performance in the exam.

Practice questions

This book is designed to help you get better results.

- Study the grade A and C candidates' answers, and see if you could have done better.
- Try the exam practice questions, and then check the answers.
- Make sure you understand why the answers given are correct.
- When you feel ready, try the AS and A2 mock exam papers.

If you perform well on the questions in this book, you should do well in the examination.

Planning and timing your answers in the exams

- You should spend the first few minutes of the assessment reading through the whole question paper.
- When answering structured questions, do not feel that you have to complete one part before starting the next. The further you are into a question, the more difficult the marks can be to obtain. If you run out of ideas, go on to the next part/question.
- You need to respond to as many parts of questions as possible. You will not score well if you spend so long trying to perfect the first questions that you do not reach later questions at all.
- Use the mark allocation to guide you on how much to write, and on how many different points to make.
- Plan your answers: don't write down the first thing that comes into your head.
- Make sure your plan reminds you to refer to any relevant information in the given case study/situation.
- Make sure you give a balanced answer where required.
- Allow some time at the end to read through your answers.

How to boost your grade

Organisation

- Organise your main and revision notes carefully, keeping them in a file.
- If you use highlighter pens or underlining to emphasise sections of your notes, make sure you limit their use to the really important points.

Research

- Spend some time reading the 'broadsheet' papers or other sources of up-to-date business information.
- Make brief summaries of business developments: you may be able to mention these developments when answering the exam questions.
- This research will also help you with coursework projects.

Answering the question

- Make sure you read and study the data before you tackle the questions.
- You'll rarely find that a question is one-sided in outcome, so always give a balanced answer/conclusion.
- Keep referring back to the question for information you may need to extract or comment on in your answer.
- If you decide to start by answering the question you think you can do best first, don't spend over-long on this question because you will lose valuable time needed to construct answers to the other questions.

Words and figures

- Marks are not only given for correct spelling, punctuation and grammar: you'll score higher marks if you can use business terms and language suitably.
- Study and become familiar with the key terms used in the main functional areas: marketing, accounting, human resource management and production.
- Be particularly careful when using accounting terms: for example, profit and cash are different, and so are profit and profitability.
- You should make sure that your answer is clear, easy to read and concise
- If possible, estimate any numerical answer first.
- Check any calculations you have made, and make sure that your answer is sensible. Is it given in the correct units (eg £000)? Does it look right?

Diagrams and formulae

- Check whether you will be given formulae in the exam, eg for standard deviation or time series calculations. If so, you don't need to waste time memorising them BUT you still need to understand how the formula is constructed, why it exists and what it calculates.
- You should make sure that any graphs, charts or other diagrams are correctly labelled, given a relevant heading, and have a suitable scale that fills (most of) the graph paper.

Questions with model answers

C grade candidate – mark scored 15/30

 For help see Revise AS Study Guide pp. 26–29, 32–40, 52–58

Examiner's Commentary

NICDR Ltd is a manufacturer of CD ROMs. It took part in an IDB trade mission 18 months ago and, as a result, is now exporting to the Middle East. Sales are good but there are many problems involved in transporting goods from Northern Ireland to the Middle East. For this reason NICDR Ltd is considering setting up a manufacturing base in Dubai, in the Middle East.

NICDR Ltd is currently involved in discussions with Acorba, a small manufacturer of CD ROMs already established in Dubai. Acorba would favour a joint venture arrangement but NICDR Ltd would prefer to either establish its own new factory and manufacture the CD ROMs in Dubai or take over Acorba as an overseas subsidiary and carry out the manufacturing there.

(a) Outline the meaning of the following terms:

    (i) 'multinational'   **[2]**

    (ii) 'joint venture'   **[2]**

    (iii) 'trade mission'   **[2]**

    (iv) 'subsidiary'   **[2]**

(b) **(i)** Explain how IDB trade missions can benefit such firms as NICDR Ltd.   **[6]**

'IDB' refers to Industrial Development Board.

    (ii) Suggest reasons why NICDR Ltd might decide to expand its international operations by manufacturing in its own factory in Dubai rather than agreeing to a joint venture with Acorba.   **[4]**

(c) Evaluate the impact on Dubai of NICDR Ltd deciding to set up its own new factory in that country.   **[12]**

[CCEA 2000 paper 1]

(a) (i) This is a firm with branches in another country ✔.

(ii) Firms agree to work together to make profits, but they also have to share costs ✔.

Limited descriptions/ definitions, and (i) is an incomplete definition of a multinational.

(iii) A government body goes abroad in an attempt to win trade for its economy ✔.

(iv) A firm that is owned by another firm ✔.

(b) (i) A trade mission will organise matters for a company such as NICDR Ltd ✔. *As a result, the company finds it a lot easier to deal with overseas organisations* ✔, *because it can rely on the trade mission to establish links* ✔.

Questions with model answers

C grade candidate continued

For help see Revise AS Study Guide pp. 26–29, 32–40, 52–58

(ii) The benefit to NICDR Ltd is that it will remain in full control of the work ✔. Its own managers can take all the decisions, and work exclusively for the benefit of NICDR Ltd ✔.

(c) Dubai will gain through having an additional firm in its economy, which will be bringing in advanced technology and working arrangements ✔. This will stimulate the economy, and help develop this CD ROM industry, which will in time lead to exports ✔. The problems that Dubai will face include a possible increase in home-based employment, and the fact that NICDR Ltd can withdraw from the country when it likes ✔. Since NICDR Ltd is in control of its own affairs, it can also `export´ its profits, if it gains financially by doing so (e.g. through a better tax regime in the UK) ✔. Some multinationals have exploited overseas economies and created pollution, and NICDR could possibly do this ✔, which would again disadvantage Dubai.

It is likely that Dubai can survive without NICDR, especially since it is an oil-rich country, and it may be better not to let too many multinationals dominate its economy ✔.

Examiner's Commentary

The answer to part (ii) is rather brief, and – although it contains key phrases such as 'full control' and 'work exclusively' – one point only is being made.

There are some strong arguments presented against NICDR, though these are not fully developed, and some important arguments in favour of its presence in Dubai are ignored. A more balanced answer should have been presented.

A grade candidate – mark scored 29/30

(a) (i) A multinational is a business with its headquarters in one country, but with manufacturing or assembly plants in at least one other ✔ ✔.

(ii) A joint venture takes place when (at least) two firms set up a division that will be operated jointly by them ✔. They share the costs and responsibilities, and also any profits, from the joint venture ✔.

(iii) A trade mission takes place to another country, having been organised by a government department ✔ or other official body (e.g. IDB), in an attempt to boost trade through showing what that country´s firms can provide ✔.

(iv) A subsidiary is a company that, whilst normally trading under its own name, is owned by another ✔ (the holding company) through share ownership ✔ (normally 50+% of the voting shares).

(b) (i) NICDR has some experience of the value of trade missions: `as a result, it is now exporting...´. The main benefit of trade missions to NICDR is one of providing expertise and support ✔, particularly in new markets ✔ where the company has no experience. The missions give companies like NICDR the opportunity to meet potential clients, agents or distributors ✔, as well as to undertake some market research ✔. Because the missions tend to organise these trips, dealing with all the administration ✔, this proves a cost-effective way ✔ for the company to explore whether it is worthwhile exporting to, or expanding in, the market.

Brief but precise answers are needed for both marks.

A well-structured and explained answer that relates the general issues of a multinational presence to the specific situation given in the question.

Questions with model answers

A grade candidate continued

For help see Revise AS Study Guide pp. 26–29, 32–40, 52–58

Examiner's Commentary

(ii) By having their own factory, NICDR will be in full control of the operation. If they were in a joint venture with Acorba, the responsibility for the operation would have to be shared: as a result, decisions could take longer to make and to implement, potentially leading to a loss of competitiveness ✔ ✔.

Furthermore, in the joint venture the firms would share the profits: if NICDR retains control, it keeps all profits itself ✔. These profits might well be higher due to the quicker decision-making, although NICDR may at first lack direct local contact with the market ✔, compared with working more closely with Acorba, and this might reduce profits to start with.

Part (ii) of the question asks for 'reasons', so at least two reasons explained in some detail – as here – are required.

(c) The benefits to Dubai are likely to include a higher level of gross national product as a result of more employment. The standard of living will therefore rise ✔. The fact that more CD ROMs are likely to be produced may lead to exports from Dubai, which would improve its balance of payments through more exports (also possibly fewer imports, if production increases and can satisfy home demand for CD ROMs) ✔ ✔. Having a new factory in Dubai should bring new, efficient work practices into the country, and create additional competition for local firms: this should improve efficiency overall, thereby making the country's economy that much more competitive ✔ ✔.

However, as a multinational with its headquarters overseas, NICDR is in a position to act in its own interests rather than those of Dubai. One example here is that NICDR may decide to move its profits out of Dubai if it can save tax by doing so ✔ ✔. A second cause for concern will arise if there is damage to the local environment, e.g. from the manufacturing process ✔ ✔. Also, it is likely that the local competition stimulated by NICDR will lead to closures of some Dubai-based firms, possibly creating high local unemployment ✔ ✔.

On balance, I think that NICDR's presence in Dubai is likely to prove beneficial, especially since it is a 'high-tech' company bringing up-to-date technological expertise into the country, which will have a 'knock-on' effect.

A well-structured and properly explained answer that relates the general issues of a multinational presence to the specific situation given in the question.

Exam practice questions

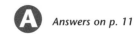 *Answers on p. 11*

Read the following passage and then answer the question that follows.

(1) Business failures in Wales in 1999 increased by 26% when compared with the previous year. Late payment, according to Dun and Bradstreet's business information survey, is a major factor and the worst-hit victims are likely to be the small firms.

Source: adapted from *The Western Mail*, 5 January 2000

Discuss the view that there is no future for small businesses in the United Kingdom economy. **[11]**

[WJEC 2000 Module 4]

Answer

The limitations of small firms are well known: difficulty in raising finance, lack of specialist expertise, few if any economies of scale. Yet small firms remain the dominant form of business organisation in the UK economy.

This is largely due to one or more of these reasons.
- Their willingness to provide products that larger firms don't wish to supply: examples include supplying components for a large firm, or a specialist service such as providing foodstuffs or cleaning services.
- They may operate in a specific niche or specialist market with local/limited demand: examples include 'collector' firms (e.g. stamp and model collecting), and local shops such as hairdressers or specialist foodstuffs.
- They may provide a particular skill that is best suited to small-scale operation or that meets limited demand: (e.g. local accountants and estate agents).
- Simply as a result of being small, these firms are often better able to adapt quickly to changing market conditions.

Assuming these conditions continue to exist in the UK economy – the need for specialists, the existence of small-scale or local demand – then there is no reason why small firms cannot continue to flourish.

Examiner's tip

To gain most of the 11 marks available, you should give specific examples of situations where small firms continue to thrive.

Questions with model answers

C grade candidate – mark scored 14/29

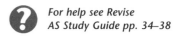

For help see Revise
AS Study Guide pp. 34–38

	Examiner's Commentary

VIRGIN GROUP GOES PUBLIC

After the flotation in 1987, Richard Branson held 55% of the Virgin Group; the outside investors held 34%. Each share had been sold at 140 pence so that Virgin Group plc was valued at £240 million.

Most people think that 50% of a public company is the key to controlling it. While this is true in theory, to a large extent control is lost just by having to appoint non-executive directors and generally giving up time to satisfy the City. During the year that flotation took place, Virgin was arguably less creative than ever. At least 50% of the time was spent heading off to the City to explain what the company was doing to fund managers, financial advisers and City PR firms, rather than just getting on and doing it.

Richard Branson was reluctant to follow British tradition and pay out a large dividend. He preferred the American or Japanese tradition whereby a company concentrates on reinvesting its profits to build itself and increase share value.

Source: adapted from Losing my Virginity: The Autobiography
by Richard Branson (Virgin Publishing, 2000)

(a) Briefly explain how a public limited company differs from a private limited company. **[4]**

(b) Discuss how Virgin's stakeholders may be affected by the switch to becoming a public limited company? **[10]**

(c) In 1988, Richard Branson decided to change the company back to a private limited company, with the financial help of Japanese investors. Discuss the benefits to be gained from this decision. **[15]**

(a) Public limited companies can sell their shares to the public and will be found on the Stock Exchange ✔. *They must have £50 000-worth of shares. Private limited companies are usually family-owned and family-run* ✔.

Some basic knowledge but not very clearly expressed. It is a __minimum__ of £50 000 of shares.

(b) Stakeholders include shareholders, employees, suppliers, customers and the community. The community is a stakeholder because the company will create jobs in the area and provide business for other local firms. However, a company can also create problems because of pollution. By becoming a public limited company, Virgin will probably get bigger, which may provide more jobs but will also cause more pollution ✔.

Good start by clearly showing who stakeholders are.

Employees may gain better job security ✔, *but will now be part of a bigger organisation and so become more of a "name and number", whereas before they felt more a part of the company* ✔.

Questions with model answers

C grade candidate continued

For help see Revise
AS Study Guide pp. 34–38

The new shareholders will benefit from the flotation, because they will now get a share of Virgin's profits although Richard Branson will get to keep less ✔. The suppliers may now feel safer dealing with a bigger more financially sound company ✔. The customers may benefit from lower prices ✔.

c) Turning the company back into a private limited company means that Richard Branson will not have to give any profits to shareholders ✔. He will be able to reinvest profits into new ideas for the future, which will be good for the company ✔.

He will be able to make decisions without having to explain them to people in the City ✔, and the time he has been spending doing this can be spent more profitably ✔. Virgin will also be able to ensure that they do not lose control of the company ✔ and can keep more financial information secret, as company reports do not have to be made public ✔.

Examiner's Commentary

If the answer had made better use of the evidence in the case study and evaluated the issues it would have gained more marks.

Discuss means that the examiners want you to present a reasoned argument, examining different points of view. You need to use the context and for top marks come to a reasoned decision. See page 13 of Revise AS Business Studies for more detail about what different words used by examiners mean.

A grade candidate – mark scored 27/29

(a) A public limited company is able to advertise and sell its shares to the public ✔, whereas a private limited company can only sell its shares privately to friends and family ✔. Also, shares of private limited companies can only be transferred or sold with the other shareholders' permission ✔. The public limited company's shares may be quoted on the Stock Market, with a minimum share capital of £50 000 ✔.

(b) One group of stakeholders greatly affected by the change are the owners. The main owner before flotation was Richard Branson himself, along with a number of friends and family. During this time the profits made were reinvested and not distributed to the owners. Now as a public limited company, some of its profits will have to be distributed to the shareholders to ensure that they are kept happy and remain as shareholders ✔. If the shareholders are not satisfied with the size of the dividend, they may sell their shares, so reducing the price of the shares and hence the value of the company ✔. Alternatively, they may take their complaints to the AGM, leading to bad publicity ✔.

Clear reaction by the shareholders is analysis, which is awarded with more than half marks.

As well as dividends the flotation of the company causes a divorce between ownership and control ✔. Although Richard Branson is still the majority shareholder, he has to bear in mind other shareholders when decisions are made. The fact that he had to spend 50% of his time visiting these other shareholders is evidence that they have to be kept informed ✔.

This paragraph shows good links between theory and the use of evidence from the case study.

Questions with model answers

A grade candidate continued

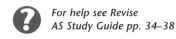

*For help see Revise
AS Study Guide pp. 34–38*

The banks, as a stakeholder, may benefit from the decision to float the company. As the company will now have greater equity as a source of capital, the debt provided by the bank will make up a smaller and less risky proportion of Virgin's finance ✔.

Customers may find that they are now being less well served by the public limited company ✔. As Richard Branson declares himself, the year after flotation saw less creativity taking place, which is what Virgin are famous for ✔. If less time is being spent on new ideas then arguably the customers will not be getting a constant supply of new and better products ✔.

To gain 9 or 10 marks this candidate's answer would need to show the potential conflict that exists in trying to satisfy different shareholders.

(c) Whilst it is a public limited company with shareholders, a business like Virgin is at the mercy of the City and must do everything to keep the City happy ✔. The distribution of dividends is expected and, as stated in the article, is relatively high in the UK. This money may be better reinvested into a growing company such as Virgin ✔. By returning to being a private limited company Virgin can concentrate again on the most important aspect of running a business - namely, producing new products of a high quality ✔.

Another problem of being a public limited company is that factors outside the company's control can have a major effect. Lack of confidence in the stock market may lead to a large fall in share prices of all companies ✔. In this case, the value of Virgin will fall by many millions of pounds ✔. This will have serious effects on the financing of the firm, if it has debt secured against the company's balance sheet ✔. If the company is now worth less because of a stock market crash, it may be forced to cut its borrowing ✔ or find that the banks, to compensate for the higher risk, increase the cost of borrowing ✔.

The City is mainly interested in the short-term performance of a company ✔. For a company such as Virgin involved in many different industries - many at their early stage of development such as the airline, mobile phones and finance - the short-term returns may be poor ✔. This may reduce the attractiveness of Virgin shares and so push down their value ✔.

The candidate makes a clearly evaluative comment to guarantee high marks.

I assume that when Richard Branson made the decision to buy back the shares he took these factors into account. Although the extra finance available from being a public limited company is helpful ✔, it may well have been at the expense of having to pander to the fund managers and financial advisers ✔, seeing profits leaking out of the company and accepting that the public success of the company is affected by factors outside its control or influence ✔.

A common way to answer a question about the benefits of making a decision is to outline the problems with the alternative, or of not making that decision.

Exam practice questions

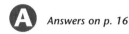

Answers on p. 16

(1) Southern Foods plc is a large company with interests in food processing and the retail trade. Its directors are devising a new mission statement based on a draft submitted by the company's managing director. In its current mission statement the company seeks 'honourably to serve the needs of the community by providing products and services of superior quality at a fair price to all our customers'. The draft of the new mission statement includes references to environmental concerns and to stakeholders other than customers.

(a) Explain what is meant by a mission statement. **[2]**

(b) Suggest and justify amendments to the mission statement which might refer to a stakeholder other than a customer. **[9]**

Source: Edexcel AS Speciment Paper – Unit 1 (Question 1a & b)

(2) **British Gas Chief Receives 75% Pay Rise**

Mr Cedric Brown, chief executive of British Gas, has received a 75% pay rise taking his basic annual salary to £475 000. This pay rise makes Mr Brown's basic pay amongst the highest of any UK public company director. The news has provoked an angry reaction from trade unions and polticians. Mr David Stirzaker, a senior official of Unison, Britain's largest trade union, said that Unison members who worked at British Gas had received rises of less than 3%.

British Gas said that the review by the company's remuneration committee, composed of non-executive directors, concluded that its directors were underpaid in comparison with other British based international companies.

The company added, 'we are expanding internationally and need to recruit, retain and motivate top calibre international management.'

The executive directors said that from next year the company's annual report and accounts would contain far greater details of each director's salary package, including perks such as company cars.

Source: adapted from the *Financial Times*, 21 November, 1994

(a) Give **three** examples of groups which are stakeholders in a business. **[3]**

(b) Discuss the extent to which shareholders could have power to reverse the decisions of the non-executive directors. **[6]**

[AQA Specimen Paper 1997 – Paper 1 (Question 6 a & b)]

Answers

(1) (a)   Suggested definition: A document that sets out the company's aims, priorities and values in a way that can be understood by all stakeholders.

(b)   Reference could be made to a number of different stakeholders. The most likely to be included are:
- Employees – to be a fair and understanding employer.
- Suppliers – to have fair dealings with suppliers, paying invoices promptly and offering a fair price.
- Shareholders – to pay a reasonable dividend and to keep them informed of relevant dealings.
- The community – to be responsible in all dealings with the local community, concerning the disposal of waste, the creation of noise and involvement with local groups.

Examiner's tip

Although the question only refers to a stakeholder, it is unlikely that you could gain 9 marks from discussing just the one. It is better to mention two or three, which will allow you briefly to mention the potential conflict between stakeholders.

(2) (a)   Any three from:
- Shareholders;
- Employees;
- Customers;
- Investors;
- The Community;
- Suppliers.

(b)
- In theory the shareholders are the owners of the company and have the authority to manage the company.
- In practice the shareholders of most companies have too little power individually.
- Shareholders have to approve new directors and their pay rises, but in practice as very few actually attend AGM's or even vote, they generally rubber-stamp decisions made by the Board of Directors.

Questions with model answers

C grade candidate – mark scored 15/30

 For help see AS Study Guide pp. 50–51

Robert Short is the recently appointed Managing Director of Bakers plc, a biscuit manufacturer employing one hundred and fifty workers. He is concerned about sales and profits and is keen to introduce performance-related pay for all workers in the firm. In order to test reactions to this he asked a number of managers to seek out opinions informally among the workers. Not everyone was pleased at the suggestion.

Production workers felt that they would earn more from such a scheme. On the other hand, the sales team, who have always earned more than production workers, feared that performance-related pay, combined with growing competition in the biscuit market, could leave them worse off.

When Robert took over as Managing Director his salary was highly publicised and this caused quite a bit of resentment among workers. Any decision he makes which affects company wages will almost certainly attract criticism.

Robert decides to push ahead with the performance-related pay scheme. His autocratic leadership style had achieved results in his previous posts. Now would be no different. He was convinced that Bakers plc would benefit in the long term.

(a) **(i)** What are the differences between formal and informal methods of communication? **[2]**

(ii) Outline **two** advantages and **two** disadvantages of using an informal method of communication in this situation. **[4]**

(b) What other strategies, apart from performance-related pay, could be employed in Bakers plc to improve the performance of the sales team? **[8]**

(c) Evaluate whether or not the Managing Director should consider changing his leadership style to one which is more democratic. **[16]**

[CCEA 2000 Paper 2]

(a) (i) Formal communication goes along the chain of command. Informal communication doesn't ✔.

(ii) Informal communication tends to be quick. Secondly, it can be helpful to some staff because the language is less formal ✔. The first disadvantage is that it is unofficial. Secondly, because it is unofficial, staff can ignore it ✔.

(b) I would suggest the firm examines the use of sales bonuses or commission. These are valuable incentives for sales staff, because they are motivated financially to sell the firm's products ✔. As a result they are likely to be happier in their work, knowing that more sales will achieve more money in their pay packets ✔. Other strategies for the firm include improving the

Examiner's Commentary

Although there are relatively few marks for (a), these answers are much too brief at AS-level: the points made need more description and explanation.

Questions with model answers

C grade candidate continued

For help see AS Study Guide pp. 50–51

Examiner's Commentary

working lot of the sales staff, e.g. taking account of what Maslow suggests is important: self-esteem and self-actualisation ✔. This means that the managers should give the sales staff the opportunity to achieve what they want to achieve, and to recognise their contributions to the work of the firm ✔.

Including references to bonuses and commissions is incorrect: the question states 'apart from performance-related pay'. Candidates who spend time including inappropriate detail penalise themselves.

(c) Many people now recognise that an autocratic approach to leadership can bring as many problems as it solves ✔. It means that the manager takes full control of the decision-making process, and this has the weakness that others are not involved ✔. Although decisions are taken quickly, the fact that the manager may not consult with others means that the decision is more likely to be a wrong one ✔. Most people enjoy taking on responsibility (e.g. McGregor and his 'Theory Y' person) ✔, and an autocratic leadership style denies them the chance ✔.

The democratic approach would involve all staff to a greater extent ✔, and support the manager's decision-making ✔, so I would support the idea of a change. Involvement means motivation, and motivation means better quality and quantity of output ✔.

The candidate has considered several implications of an autocratic leadership style, but has not realised that there are other factors that help determine the most appropriate style.

A grade candidate – mark scored 28/30

(a) (i) Formal communication takes place through the organisation's hierarchy, and is officially recognised and accepted by all staff ✔. Informal communication is unofficial, flowing 'through the grapevine' and not being formally recognised by those (especially managers) in the organisation ✔.

(ii) Two advantages are: first, that informal communication can expand and further explain a formal communication: this may be necessary in this situation ✔; second, it is an inexpensive method of communication, normally less expensive than a formal one ✔. One disadvantage is that, because it is informal, the information may become changed and inaccurate: second, it can reinforce a feeling amongst staff that management is either distant, incompetent, or both ✔.

This answer includes some of the information in the case study.

(b) In financial terms, the team could be offered additional 'perks' (fringe benefits) ✔ or, if appropriate, membership of a share scheme or profit-sharing scheme ✔, neither of which is normally classified as 'performance-related pay' at this level of employment. Management should also consider Herzberg's motivators and hygiene factors ✔, such as increasing promotion opportunities for the sales team, improvements to their work environment, and a review of their work to ensure it is interesting and motivational ✔. The status of their work should also be acknowledged, to encourage motivation ✔.

Questions with model answers

A grade candidate continued

 For help see AS Study Guide pp. 50–51

For help see AS Study Guide pp. 50–51

Examiner's Commentary

The sales team's performance could also be improved by looking `outside' their immediate department ✔. For example, a review of the firm's communication policy and procedures could improve sales performance ✔, together with an evaluation of the quality of the firm's products, an audit of the physical resources it provides for the sales team, and a review of the quality of market and other information available to them ✔.

> *A well-analysed approach, identifying a range of relevant factors.*

(c) The autocratic approach of a manager such as Robert Short has a number of advantages. It means that he retains control over decision-making ✔, which is therefore likely to be carried out quickly and consistently ✔. As a result, Bakers plc should be able to respond quickly to changing market conditions ✔.

Although Robert Short would probably find it difficult with 150 employees under him to adopt a democratic approach to leadership and management ✔, there are a number of benefits associated with the democratic approach. It is usually regarded as a more motivating leadership or management style ✔, since through greater participation in decision-making employees become more involved in the business ✔. As a result, there is improved communication, which includes effective communication of the business objectives ✔: this can also motivate employees, since they know they are involved in helping to achieve these objectives ✔. There is often less need for supervision if a democratic leadership style is adopted, with teams working more closely together towards achieving business objectives ✔.

> *The question asks for evaluation, so a balanced answer is required.*

There is no one right answer as to the style of leadership that any manager should adopt. The most appropriate style of leadership depends on a number of factors. These include the culture and history of the firm ✔ (it isn't clear whether Bakers plc has a tradition of autocratic leadership, although Robert Short was appointed presumably in the knowledge he had an autocratic style) ✔, and the manager's own personality (it is clear that Robert Short believes in the autocratic approach) ✔. Other factors include the nature and size of the staff, and the depth of the organisational structure/hierarchy: with 150 staff, the company is probably medium-sized, and seems to have a functional structure ✔.

The evidence is largely inconclusive. I would suggest that Robert Short should consider changing his style if friction continues ✔. The strengths of the democratic approach are increasingly recognised by management theorists, and to continue adopting an autocratic approach simply because it has worked in other positions is not sufficient evidence in itself that it will work in Bakers plc ✔.

> *A well-structured conclusion.*

Exam practice questions

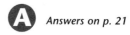

Answers on p. 21

(1) Bitza Ltd is currently producing 200 units per month. Its fixed costs are £1000 per month and its variable costs are £5.50 per unit. The table below shows its fixed and variable costs per month at five different levels of output:

OUTPUT (Units per month)	FC (£ per month)	VC (£ per month)
200	1000	1100
300	1000	1500
400	1800	2000
500	1800	2500
600	1800	2700

(i) Calculate Total Cost, Average Variable Cost and Average Cost at each level of output. **[5]**

(ii) Using your calculations and the information in the table above, examine how this firm could best gain from economies of scale. **[8]**

(iii) **(a)** Outline the ways in which Bitza Ltd may benefit from external economies of scale. **[4]**

(b) Apart from economies of scale, evaluate the impact of growth on a small business. **[13]**

[CCEA 1999 Paper 1]

Answers

(1) (i)

Output (units/month)	Fixed costs (£/month)	Variable costs (£/month)	Total costs (£/month)	Average variable costs (£/unit)	Average costs (£/unit)
200	1000	1100	2100	5.50	10.50
300	1000	1500	2500	5.00	8.33
400	1800	2000	3800	5.00	9.50
500	1800	2500	4300	5.00	8.60
600	1800	2700	4500	4.50	7.50

(ii) • Bitza Ltd gains from economies of scale at 300 units per month.
  • However, if it increases to 400/month its average costs rise to £9.50 per unit as a result of the additional £800 fixed costs (this is a 'stepped' cost).
  • Now the 'step' has occurred, presumably due to full capacity at this output, average costs again fall continually to 600 units/month (£7.50 per unit). This is due to the lower unit variable costs, e.g. through bulk-buying.
  • If the company can produce and sell at this level, it will pay to do so in terms of this cost analysis: its difficulty will be increasing its sales to match the increased output: any drop in the unit selling price may negate the benefits from lower unit costs.

(iii)(a) Bitza Ltd may gain from external economies of concentration:
  • It will benefit from having suitably skilled employees already living in the locality, nearness of support firms that supply it with its material and other requirements,
  • any positive image or reputation associated with the local area (e.g. 'Potteries china', 'Sheffield steel'),
  • local providers offering training courses relevant to its industry,
  • locally-based or locally-available sources of information and advice.

(b) Perhaps the two greatest benefits from growth are profit and recognition.
  • Profit comes from the growth in sales, assuming the business keeps its profitability (i.e. net profit margin remains roughly constant).
  • This profit will help support additional growth.
  • Recognition brings with it potential for more business in the form of extra sales/work, and – as the firm grows – this greater amount of work will require the firm to increase its productive or other capacity.
  • The greater capacity allows the firm to take on larger and more lucrative contracts.

  • Once the firm has grown beyond the accepted size of being 'small' (two from turnover above £2.8 million, balance sheet total above £1.4 million, average employees over 50), it loses exemption from filing disclosures and may also lose government help.
  • The original owners may have to relinquish some or all control due to the need for additional finance and/or a more complex organisational structure.
  • This may lead to a different organisational culture developing, and the loss of the 'personal touch' often closely associated with smaller firms.
  • Eventually the firm may reach a size at which diseconomies of scale start outweighing the economies of scale from growth.

Questions with model answers

C grade candidate – mark scored 13/26

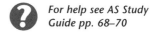

For help see AS Study Guide pp. 68–70

ICE CREAM FROM MARS

Examiner's Commentary

In the late 1980s, Walls ice cream stood as the established market leader. It must have appeared to Walls that its position could not be threatened. However, food technology was changing fast. By 1988 the market had seen the transformation of chocolate confectionery into ice cream bars; by 1995 it was the fastest growing sector of the ice cream market. Mars were the first company to launch an ice cream version of a popular chocolate bar.

However, Mars found it difficult to enter the market, as Walls and Lyons Maid were supplying freezers free of charge to small retailers on condition that they stock only their ice cream in the cabinet. The owners of Walls, Unilever, sought to prevent Mars, from entering the market and they began legal proceedings against Mars alleging that they had induced retailers to break their exclusive contracts with Walls. Eventually, Mars went to the European Commission in 1991 accusing Unilever of illegal anti-competitive practices. In October 1992, the UK's Office of Fair Trading also announced an investigation into freezer exclusivity in the UK.

In March 1994 the Monopolies and Mergers Commission found that exclusivity did not prevent competition from working. However, one year later the European Commission condemned freezer exclusivity, saying that it resulted in the restriction of competition, and so infringed Articles 85 and 86 of the EC Treaty. Eventually, the European Commission decided that the practice of freezer exclusivity was illegal throughout the EU.

Source: adapted from *The Times 100 Case Studies*, 1995 and the *Financial Times*, 10 June, 1999

(a)   Use the article to outline the role of the Monopolies and Mergers Commission (now called the Competition Commission).   **[4]**

(b)   Explain the meaning of the phrase 'restriction of competition'.   **[4]**

(c)   Analyse how the ending of freezer exclusivity may have affected Walls.   **[8]**

(d)   Discuss what other consumer protection law may affect the way in which Mars and Walls operate.   **[10]**

(a) To ensure that large companies do not exploit their customers, the Competition Commission has the power to investigate any situation where they feel that a company that has more than 25% of the market ✔, *either through growth or merger, is acting in an uncompetitive manner* ✔.

Although this is a good explanation of the role of the Competition Commission, it does not link with the evidence available in the article.

Questions with model answers

C grade candidate continued

For help see AS Study Guide pp. 68–70

Examiner's Commentary

(b) The phrase `restriction of competition´ is referring to the fact that a company can act in such a way that true competition cannot take place ✔, so affecting the consumer. In the ice cream industry there are a few large firms controlling the market ✔, so competition may be prevented ✔.

If this last comment had been explained then full marks would have been awarded.

(c) The ending of freezer exclusivity will have affected Walls in a major way. It will have meant that they faced more competition from Mars and other companies ✔. If shops are now able to put any company´s ice cream in their freezers, Walls will find that customers will have more choice when making a purchase ✔. This will mean that Walls will probably have to reduce their price to compete ✔. This will affect Walls´ position in the market, with a likely fall in market share ✔.

This is a good start to an answer, but could have so easily been developed for many more marks. What about the effect of falling sales on their profits; how may this have affected their employment levels; what might Walls have done about this?

(d) Both Mars and Walls will have to comply with many other regulations protecting the consumer ✔. One is the Trade Descriptions Act, which makes it illegal to give a wrong or misleading description of their ice cream ✔. The Food Safety Act ensures that the ice cream sold is fit for human consumption ✔. The Unsolicited Goods Act prevents consumers from demanding payment for goods received that they have not requested. The Weights and Measures Act ensures that the tubs of ice cream sold are of the correct weight ✔.

This is a poor answer, for two reasons. First, there is no direct reference to the companies in the case study. Just occasionally mentioning the words ice cream does not qualify for much context. Second, to include The Unsolicited Goods Act is nonsensical as it would be unlikely to find ice cream being sent through the post!

A grade candidate – mark scored 26/26

(a) The Competition Commission is a government organisation that checks that when legal monopolies (more than 25% of the market ✔) exist they are not against the public interest ✔. They investigated the Walls case because there may have been a case of them abusing their position in the market. It may be argued that not allowing stores to put other firms´ products into their freezers was anti-competitive ✔, as most shops would not have room to have more than one freezer and so would not be able to stock Mars´ products ✔.

The role of the Competition Commission is clearly outlined <u>and</u> is referring specifically to the context.

(b) Under UK and EU law, firms must not act in a way that prevents free competition from taking place ✔. It is expected that firms should not try to take unfair advantage of their dominant position in the market - for example, by putting undue pressure on retailers to stock their product ✔. If this is allowed to happen, the resulting lack of competition may mean that prices are higher than they should be and there will be less choice for the consumer ✔. This is likely to happen if the stores only stock Walls´ products. The lack of

Questions with model answers

A grade candidate continued

For help see AS Study Guide pp. 68–70

Examiner's Commentary

choice will adversely affect customers and will allow Walls to charge a higher price as there is little likelihood that customers will shop around for this particular product since ice cream is usually bought on impulse ✔.

Probably too full an answer for only 4 marks, but there is no doubt the student knows what they are talking about.

(c) The ending of freezer exclusivity may have had a major effect on the operation of Walls. The main effect will have been the ending of Walls' monopolistic position in the market ✔. Now that the shops can stock other brands of ice cream in their freezers, the major competitors such as Mars will have freer access to more retail outlets ✔. This will affect the sales of Walls' ice cream, as they will no longer have such guaranteed levels of sales ✔. This will potentially affect their profits ✔ and may mean that Walls will have to look at other ways of marketing their product ✔. It may also be the case that jobs will be lost within the Walls organisation, as fewer sales and support staff are needed to support lower sales output ✔.

A solid coverage of the main points so far.

However, given the fact that Walls have held such a dominant position in the market for so long, they may find that even with increased competition they are able to take advantage of the brand loyalty built up over the previous years ✔. This would suggest that as long as they still continue to provide freezers free of charge to retailers ✔, with Walls' advertising on the outside, they will only see a small fall in sales ✔.

Analysis achieved by questioning the likelihood of the most obvious scenario happening.

(d) One law that will have a huge effect on any ice cream company is the Food Safety Act ✔. It requires that food is safe for consumption, is of the quality stated and the description does not mislead the consumer ✔.

A good start. Straightaway the candidate is showing that they are only going to select the laws that affect ice cream.

For example, the freezers provided must ensure that the ice cream is kept at an appropriate temperature so that the product does not melt and potentially create health problems ✔. Also, a Lemon Sorbet lolly should actually be lemon flavoured and should be sorbet rather than ice cream ✔.

This kind of issue is also covered under the Trade Descriptions Act ✔, which requires that goods offered for sale do not have misleading descriptions ✔. An ice cream Snickers bar would be expected to contain peanuts, as they are vital ingredients in a standard Snickers chocolate bar.

The weight of an ice cream must conform to that printed on its wrapper. This is covered by the Weights and Measures Act, which makes it an offence to sell goods underweight or short in quantity ✔.

Questions with model answers

A grade candidate continued

For help see AS Study
Guide pp. 68–70

Examiner's Commentary

The failure to abide by these laws could seriously undermine the future success of Walls or Mars. The bad publicity attracted from breaking any of these laws could affect their sales. (This has happened recently to Perrier and Coca-Cola.) ✔ *It will lead to a fall in consumer confidence, which may lead to a complete collapse in demand not just for ice creams but other products as well. Both Walls and Mars are involved in many other food products, and if the consumer loses faith in one product it may lead to a fall in demand for all products made by that company. Given the fact that Walls and Mars are both operating in what is now a very competitive market, one publicised case of breaking the law may provide an opportunity for a competitor to take a larger market share, which may be very difficult to regain* ✔.

A good answer that selects the appropriate laws for this case and then discusses the implications of not abiding by them. Good recognition that any slip-up by Mars or Walls will have a potential long-term effect in such a competitive market.

Exam practice questions

Answers on p. 28

DECISION TIME AT J & M TAYLOR

J & M Taylor Ltd is a family-run business based in the north east of England. The business is still owned and run by the founders, John and Mary Taylor. Their two children, Robert and Joanne, joined the business after leaving university in 1990 and 1993 respectively. In addition to the four family members, the business also employs 12 other people who are employed in the production of the various products on which the business has built its reputation over the last 20 years.

The business is a supplier of ingredients, such as buns, salads, and potatoes, required by the fast food industry. From the start, it has been company policy to supply a large range of products in order that they could appeal to as wide a customer base as possible. This policy has been very successful so far and the company supplies a wide variety of outlets, varying from fish and chip shops to the more fashionable types of outlet such as tapas bars.

The North East has recently experienced the loss of a large number of jobs in the textile and electronics industries pushing the unemployment rate in the area to approximately 8%. Many people in the region were beginning to economise and were cutting down on any unnecessary expenditure. One of the sectors feeling the pressure from such cuts was the take-away food industry with most outlets reporting a noticeable drop in trade. J & M Taylor Ltd was no exception; over the last eight weeks Robert had reported a 10% drop in orders from regular customers.

These changes in the local economy have led the family to consider setting up a totally new business that would, hopefully, take advantage of the current fashion for eating organic food. They were considering calling this new venture 'Freshers' and its mission would be to provide high quality snacks using only organic produce. Joanne had been consciously buying organic food whenever she could for almost five years now and was therefore aware of the range of food that was available and its price. She had done some market research and had found that there was not a single cafe in the area that was offering organic food. Therefore she was convinced that although the take-away and cafe businesses in the region were seeing a downturn in sales, a new venture promising only pure and wholesome food would attract sufficient people to make the business profitable. Her main problem was that she needed to persuade the rest of the family that setting up a new business at this time was not foolish and was likely to succeed. She emphasised that, although the business cycle was experiencing a downturn at the moment, the family should be prepared for the upturn which would, hopefully, follow.

The family decided to hold a business meeting to discuss the options open to them in order to ensure the company's survival. Robert suggested that before the meeting each of them should do a SWOT analysis of the business and they would then have a foundation on which to base their discussion.

During the meeting it became clear that they had two main options available to them. They could reduce their workforce until demand began to increase again or they could try Joanne's idea and start a new business based on organic snacks. They agreed to go away and to meet again in three days when each of them would have prepared a list of the advantages and disadvantages of both of the proposals.

Exam practice questions

When they met again Mary shocked them all by saying that she had not bothered to consider the two options because, after leaving the first meeting, she had thought of an even better idea. She said that she was convinced that they should concentrate on the business that they have been successful in for the past 20 years and that, instead of risking a totally new business, they should explore the possibility of exporting the products that they currently make and supply. She argued that the reduction in interest rates made this the ideal time for such an experiment. As Mary had not been known for coming up with ideas in the past, she was rather surprised when John, Robert and Joanne all agreed that this was something that could be worth considering. Now they had three options to consider!

During the same period that the job losses and the fall in orders were occurring, interest rates were reduced by a total of 0.75% from 7% to 6.25%. This was thought to be in response to appeals from businesses which said that they could not afford to invest at the higher rates of interest, and that the exchange rate was being pushed up and was reducing their ability to gain export orders.

[AQA AS specimen paper – Unit 3 (Questions 2 & 5)]

(a) Explain two ways in which a fall in interest rates can affect a business such as J & M Taylor Ltd. **[10]**

(b) Evaluate the business opportunities for J & M Taylor Ltd resulting from a future upturn in the business cycle. **[18]**

Answers

(a)   Possible ways that a lower interest rate may affect the business:
- The cost of loans taken out by J & M Taylor Ltd will fall. This will make the cost of developing the organic concept or exporting sides of the business cheaper and therefore more attractive.
- Cheaper to invest in new equipment or products. Again, this makes the proposed plans cheaper and more attractive.
- Consumers will have more money to spend as the fall in interest rates will reduce the cost of mortgage payments and hire purchase. This may lead to an upturn in demand for the core products.
- Not as expensive to hold stocks – therefore production may increase to replenish stocks that have been allowed to dwindle during periods of high interest rates.

(b)   An upturn in the business cycle will create the following opportunities:
- Increase in orders from existing customers as demand picks up. More fast food outlets are likely to open so that new customers will be created.
- A growth in income and demand will create opportunities for new products to be introduced, such as the organic range.
- If the business cycle is on the upturn in other countries as well, there may be opportunities for expansion into overseas markets.
- The business may be encouraged to diversify, opening their own distribution chain.
- Increased demand without any significant price change will lead to improved profitability.
- This increased profitability will make investment in current and new lines of business more likely.

Questions with model answers

C grade candidate – mark scored 15/30

 For help see AS Study Guide pp. 76–81

Examiner's Commentary

John Andrews has been in business for three years.
The following figures were taken from his firm's balance sheet.

	£
Equipment and Fittings	2 000
Closing Stock	7 000
Debtors	1 500
Bank	500
Creditors	400
Owner's Capital	10 000
Retained Profit	600

(i)　(a) Present this information in the form of a vertical balance sheet.　　**[6]**

　　(b) Explain the term 'working capital'.　　**[2]**

　　(c) State John Andrews' working capital.　　**[1]**

　　(d) State the value of John Andrews' Net Assets.　　**[1]**

(ii)　John's accountant values his stock at cost price but John wants to value his stock at selling price. Use your knowledge and understanding of current accounting concepts and standards to advise John if valuing stock at selling price is acceptable.　　**[6]**

(iii)　Evaluate the usefulness of final accounts to the various stakeholders of a public limited company.　　**[14]**

[CCEA 1999 Paper 1]

(i) (a) <u>Balance Sheet</u>　　　　　£　　　　　£

　　　<u>Fixed assets</u>

　　　　Equipment and fittings　　　2 000　✔

　　　<u>Current assets</u>

　　　　Stocks　　　　7 000

　　　　Debtors　　　1 500

　　　　Bank　　　　　500

　　　　　　　　　　9 000　✔

　　　<u>Current liabilities</u>

　　　　Creditors　　　400　✔

　　　　　　　　　　　　　　8 600

　　　　　　　　　　　　　10 600　✔

　　Capital　　　　　　　　10 000

　　Profit　　　　　　　　　600

　　　　　　　　　　　　　10 600　✔

(b) 'Working capital' is current assets less current liabilities ✔*.*

The heading should read 'Balance Sheet as at . . .'

Although accurate, some labelling is abbreviated or omitted, notably the name of the owner and the descriptions 'net current assets' and 'net assets'.

The candidate hasn't explained what working capital is, but has simply stated how it is calculated.

Questions with model answers

C grade candidate continued

For help see AS Study Guide pp. 76–81

Examiner's Commentary

(c) John Andrews has £8 600 working capital ✔.

(d) Net assets are £9 000.

> This is incorrect: the candidate has selected 'current assets' in error.

(ii) This means John Andrews will be accepting that profit has been made before the stock is sold ✔. *This is not allowed by prudence* ✔, *which is one of the accounting concepts. As a result, John Andrews cannot value his stock at selling price because there is no guarantee it will be sold* ✔.

> An accurate, but limited, statement. There is no mention of SSAP 9, and the prudence concept has not been explained fully.

(iii) The main stakeholders for public limited companies are interested in two main aspects of the company: its profits and its liquidity. The final accounts are the profit and loss account and balance sheet, and between them these show profit and liquidity (for example, working capital).

Profits are important when the stakeholders want to check the value of their investment ✔, *or whether they are going to get a good return as dividend or interest payments* ✔. *Liquidity will be important to stakeholders lending money to the plc* ✔, *because they will want their money back at some stage* ✔. *They will also want the plc to make profits, because they want to be paid interest* ✔.

> 'Profit' is mentioned, but stakeholders are normally more interested in measuring profit against capital employed or turnover, i.e. 'profitability' for the plc. Stakeholders are not identified: this omission makes producing a structured and logical answer more difficult.

A grade candidate – mark scored 29/30

(i) (a) John Andrews: Balance Sheet as at . . . . . ✔

	£	£
Fixed assets		
Equipment and fittings		2 000 ✔
Current assets		
Stocks	7 000	
Debtors	1 500	
Bank	500	
	9 000 ✔	
Current liabilities		
Creditors	400 ✔	
Net current assets		8 600
Net assets		10 600 ✔
Financed by:		
Owner's capital		10 000
Net profit		600
		10 600 ✔

> This is a more fully labelled Balance Sheet.

(b) 'Working capital' is the excess of current assets over current liabilities ✔, *and indicates John's ability to meet short-term debts as they fall due* ✔.

> The question asks for an explanation, not merely a statement of how working capital is calculated.

Questions with model answers

A grade candidate continued

For help see AS Study Guide pp. 76–81

Examiner's Commentary

(c) John has £8 600 working capital: £9 000 current assets - £400 current liabilities ✔.

Good, workings are shown: this is always important with numerical questions.

(d) Net assets are £10 600 ✔.

Following the vertical layout gives this answer, as well as that to (i) (c).

(ii) John cannot value stock at selling price, because this is against the concept of prudence (sometimes known as conservatism) ✔. This concept states that, where different valuations are possible, a business must select the one giving the most cautious presentation of its financial state ✔. This basically means `always anticipate a loss but never anticipate a profit`. This is reinforced by SSAP 9 ✔, which states that stock should be valued at the lower of cost or net realisable value ✔. This means, therefore, that John Andrews will not be allowed to value his stock at selling price, because it would be anticipating a profit, and is also not allowed by SSAP 9 ✔.

The candidate might also have added a comment that profits are only recognised when they are actually made – i.e. when the stock is sold.

(iii) A plc has many stakeholders. Some of these are internal to the firm - for example, the employees and managers - and others are external. External stakeholders include shareholders, the government (e.g. HM Customs & Excise in connection with VAT), customers, suppliers and lenders ✔ ✔. Internally, employees will be interested in the plc's liquidity ✔, since it needs sufficient liquid assets to survive and employ staff ✔. They may also be interested in its profitability ✔, especially if they have a direct interest, e.g. through a profit-sharing scheme ✔. Managers will also be interested in liquidity, as well as judging its success internally (i.e. checking profitability or other trends against past accounting records) and externally (assessing performance against competitors): the final accounts form the basis for this analysis ✔ ✔.

Classifying stakeholders as 'internal' and 'external' has helped to structure the answer.

Externally, shareholders will be interested in the plc's profitability and overall performance, since this affects (a) the share price ✔ and (b) the amount of dividend they will receive ✔. Shareholders use final accounts to judge whether their investment remains worthwhile. Lenders such as banks or debenture holders will want to reassure themselves that their investment in the plc is safe: the evidence comes from analysing its final accounts to see whether it is in a position to pay interest, and also to repay the loans ✔ ✔. Suppliers will check the final accounts to assess working capital levels, again to see whether the plc is in a position to pay them ✔.

The above illustrates that final accounts will be of great interest to all stakeholders of a plc, although the focus of this interest will vary from stakeholder to stakeholder ✔.

The opening statement sets the scene by identifying a suitable range of stakeholders, and the final comment summarises and answers the question.

Exam practice questions

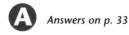

Answers on p. 33

(1) Dargon Distribution is owned by John Shah. John has just completed his first year of trading and his sister, Velma, is going to help him with his first set of final accounts. Dargon Distribution owns two main fixed assets. Velma has asked John to estimate the working life of each asset and what the scrap value of each might be at the end of that time. John's estimates are set out in the table below.

	Cost Price	Working Life (years)	Estimated Scrap Value
Van	£6 000	3	£3 000
Computer	£2 100	5	£680

(i) Define the term 'depreciation'. **[2]**

(ii) Using **both** the Straight Line and Reducing Balance (at 20%) methods:

    (a) Calculate the depreciation which would be charged each year of the life of each asset. **[4]**

    (b) Indicate the net book value at the end of each year of each asset's life. **[4]**

    (c) State which method of depreciation John should use, and why. **[2]**

(iii) Evaluate the impact on Dargon Distribution of a decision by John to ignore the depreciation of his fixed assets. **[18]**

[CCEA 2000 Paper 1]

Answers

(1) **(i)** The fall in value of a fixed asset over a period of time (its useful life), e.g. due to wear and tear, obsolescence or depreciation.

(ii)(a) and **(b)** Straight line (Van)

Year	Book value at start	Depreciation	Book value at end
1	6 000	1 000	5 000
2	5 000	1 000	4 000
3	4 000	1 000	3 000

Straight line (Computer)

Year	Book value at start	Depreciation	Book value at end
1	2 100	284	1 816
2	1 816	284	1 532
3	1 532	284	1 248
4	1 248	284	964
5	964	284	680

Reducing balance (Van)

Year	Book value at start	Depreciation	Book value at end
1	6 000	1 200	4 800
2	4 800	960	3 840
3	3 840	768	3 072

Reducing balance (Computer)

Year	Book value at start	Depreciation	Book value at end
1	2 100	420	1 680
2	1 680	336	1 344
3	1 344	268.80	1 075.20
4	1 075.20	215.04	860.16
5	860.16	172.03	688.13

(c) • Both straight line and reducing balance are acceptable methods.
- The advantage of using reducing balance is that the amounts charged for depreciation in the earlier years are higher, and more representative of the true loss in value of vehicles and computers.

(iii) • Failure to depreciate fixed assets means that John will not be showing a 'true and fair view' of his fixed assets in the balance sheet.
- As a result, the fixed assets will be overvalued.
- The yearly depreciation charge is also shown in the profit & loss account as a charge against gross profit: as a result, John's net profit will also be shown at too high an amount.
- This means John will pay more tax on the profits than necessary.
- When the assets are disposed of, a substantially lower profit figure for the year in which they are sold would be produced.
- By not depreciating his fixed assets, John is also ignoring the accruals (matching) concept, expenses are allocated to the year to which they refer: depreciation is an attempt to share the assets' cost across all the years for which the assets are held.

Examiner's tip

You need to refer to the effect of depreciating assets in both the profit & loss account and the balance sheet. You should also mention the effect of non-depreciation when the fixed assets are eventually sold.

Questions with model answers

C grade candidate – mark scored 15/31

For help see AS Study Guide
pp. 93–94 & 98–100

Sena Sikata and Richard Elliott had been the Joint Managing Directors of a Young Enterprise Company during their time at school five years ago. They had run a 'company' providing marketing services to local businesses. After leaving school they had decided to set up a 'real' company and chose to set up a business that provided administration services such as report binding and business stationery. It had proved to be fairly successful. However, although business was good and profits were high, they had always had problems with labour turnover, as shown by the following table.

LENGTH OF SERVICE	NUMBER OF EMPLOYEES
More than 1 year	2
6 months – 1 year	4
3 months – 6 months	4
Less than 3 months	6

(a) Outline what is meant by the phrase 'Labour Turnover'.   **[3]**

(b) Calculate the Annual Labour Turnover implied by the table.   **[3]**

(c) Evaluate how Sena and Richard might deal with the problems created by the high labour turnover.   **[15]**

(d) Discuss the legal issues related to employment that Richard and Sena might need to consider when setting up a 'real' company.   **[10]**

(a) Labour turnover is the number of people who leave a company in a year ✔.

(b) Turnover = 14 ✗

(c) The high labour turnover may be caused by the fact that the jobs are boring and badly paid ✔. *It may be that the workers who have been recruited in the past have been poorly chosen, so that they have not fitted in to the company or been unable to do the job very well* ✔. *The workers may feel unappreciated and decide to go and work elsewhere.*

The workers need to be better motivated ✔. *Maslow says that workers need to have their basic needs satisfied first, with a decent wage, but then want security needs and friendship needs* ✔. *Maybe these are not being met. It is very unlikely that they will be able to obtain esteem and self-actualisation needs in this sort of job* ✔.

Taylor said that money was the only motivator. So maybe the workers should be paid more. Could they be given more responsibility or promotion to follow what Herzberg believed? Maybe the management style of Sena and Richard is

Examiner's Commentary

Labour turnover must be calculated relative to the size of the workforce. The number of people leaving Sainsburys in a year will be more than at the local bakers. But this does not mean that the baker's labour turnover is lower.

The question does not ask for the causes of the problem. They are worth mentioning briefly if you are then going to link them with how to resolve them. But this answer does not do that.

Why not?

C grade candidate continued

 For help see AS Study Guide pp. 93–94 & 98–100

Examiner's Commentary

not very good ✔. They might be too autocratic or too laissez-faire ✔. Sena and Richard should read about Douglas McGregor's X and Y theory. They certainly need to do something about the high labour turnover because it will be costing them money ✔.

> *This answer shows excellent knowledge of the relevant theory. It is a shame that it has not been better linked with the information about the company.*

(d) There are lots of laws that will affect the business. For example, a fairly new law is the Working Time Regulations 1998, brought in as part of the UK's acceptance of The Social Charter ✔. This means that all workers are entitled to four weeks' paid holiday a year, one day's rest a week and a maximum average of 48 hours work a week ✔. The Health & Safety Act 1974 ensures that all employees are able to work in a safe working environment ✔. Every employer must produce a written document about health and safety. Larger firms must have an accident book and a trained First Aider ✔. If a company does not abide by the law they may be fined or taken to court ✔.

> *This is not a Law AS level. Detailed knowledge about dates and titles of the legislation is far less important than recognising how the law affects a business.*

The firm must also abide by The Disability Discrimination Act 1995, The Race Relations Act 1976 and The Sex Discrimination Act 1975 ✔. This means that Sena and Richard cannot refuse to employ someone because of the colour of their skin, their sex or a disability.

Other laws that must be followed are those that say all workers must have a written contract ✗.

> *Not actually what the law says.*

A grade candidate – mark scored 29/31

(a) This is the rate at which employees leave a company ✔, usually expressed as a percentage for the year ✔. It can be calculated using the formula:

$$\text{Labour Turnover} = \frac{\text{Number of workers leaving a firm in one year}}{\text{Average number of staff employed in a year}} \times 100 ✔$$

(b) Labour Turnover $= 14/16 \times 100$
$= 87.5\%$ ✔ ✔ ✔

> *If 14 employees have been with the company for less than one year it is fair to assume that they have replaced 14 workers who have left in the last year.*

(c) With such a high labour turnover it would appear that this company has a serious problem with retaining its staff, although it would be useful to be able to compare this figure with the industry average. The nature of the job will be mainly unskilled, which is likely to attract younger workers, including students ✔. These workers are generally more mobile and are likely to move on to better jobs after a while ✔. The level of pay will obviously be important and so it would be beneficial for Sena and Richard to find out what the average wage is for this sort of work ✔. If they find that they are paying below the average then they may have to consider raising the wage rate to bring it in line with similar work ✔. This should not be too much of a problem given the fact we are told that they are very profitable ✔.

> *Good context.*

Questions with model answers

A grade candidate continued

For help see AS Study Guide pp. 93–94 & 98–100

	Examiner's Commentary

They should also consider non-financial motivational strategies ✔. There will be little scope for promotion in such a small firm and they may need to consider theorists such as Herzberg and Maslow ✔. They both suggested that needs other than money are important ✔. Greater responsibility may be a motivator, as part of job enrichment. Again, it may be difficult to enrich the type of jobs done in this company ✔. Maybe Sena and Richard should consider asking the workers for their views ✔. Not only will it help them to find out the cause of the high labour turnover, but the consultation may in itself act as a motivator ✔.

Good link between theory and practice.

Whatever the reason for the high labour turnover, it is important to deal with it. This is because it will be costing the company a lot of money in recruitment ✔ and training costs ✔. Ultimately, any extra money spent trying to resolve this problem may be less than the costs incurred if labour turnover is not reduced ✔.

Clear evaluation because the costs and benefits are weighed up.

(d) When setting up a business for real a number of legal issues related to employment are relevant. They include contracts, equal opportunities and health & safety.

Any worker employed must have a contract, with written particulars given in writing, within three months of starting work ✔. This must include things such as hours worked, holiday rights and wage rate. Since 1998 all workers must be paid at least the minimum wage, which is currently £3.70 if you are aged over 21 and £3.35 if aged between 18 and 21 ✔.

The law relating to contract of employment is confusing. Any minor errors here are less important than the general level of understanding shown.

All firms must abide by equal opportunities legislation, which covers discrimination by sex, race or disability ✔. For example, no job can be refused because of the colour of your skin or because you are a woman. However, this company will be exempt from the disability legislation because they employ fewer than 20 workers ✔. This means that they can refuse to employ a disabled worker because of the extra costs and inconvenience that it will cause - although this may be seen as unethical ✔.

A good knowledge of the law shown, with wider issues identified.

All firms, regardless of their size, are responsible for ensuring the health and safety of their employees and third parties ✔. Sena and Ricard should ensure that training is provided for using dangerous equipment, such as binding machines. The company must produce a health and safety policy and carry out regular risk assessments to minimise the chance of accidents ✔.

Failure to conform to these laws and others may lead to Sena and Richard being taken to court and/or fined ✔, which will create bad publicity and make it even more difficult to recruit and retain good workers ✔.

Exam practice questions

Answers on p. 38

(1) Read the extracts and answer *all* parts of the question which follows.

DECLINE OF FULL-TIME WORK TO CONTINUE, SAYS REPORT

As government policies to create more flexible working take effect, forecasts indicate a continuing move in the labour market away from full-time employment. This shift has greatly increased feelings of job insecurity amongst employees.

Business leaders see growth in self-employment as a clear response to trends such as job shedding. Dr Neil Blake, the report's research director, says: 'With employers creating almost no extra full-time jobs, 790 000 people will opt for self-employment between now and 2006. This enterprise activity is a positive response to the rationalisation, delayering and sub-contracting seen in many large UK firms.'

The report says that the fastest rise in employment will be for professional workers such as managers, solicitors, and accountants.

Source: adapted from Philip Bassett, Industrial Editor,
The Times, 29 October, 1996

WORK 2000: NEW EMPLOYERS

An aspect of business reality is that women are half the workforce. A smart business supports women so that they can give their maximum to the organisation. A 'shift swap' scheme at Asda, the supermarket chain, enables, for example, a female cashier to work her weekly hours and attend her son's school concert. The Midland Bank raised its retention rate for women on maternity leave from 30% to 80% by allowing them to work flexibly on their return.

Source: adapted from Jayne Buxton, *The Guardian*, 6 January, 1999

(a) What is meant by:

    (i) 'flexible working' **[2]**

    (ii) 'rationalisation' **[2]**

(b) Examine the possible disadvantages for businesses of 'increased feelings of job insecurity amongst employees'. **[7]**

(c) Many companies find that their existing employees do not have the appropriate skills for the future. Analyse how a company may overcome this problem. **[9]**

(d) To what extent would the work of motivation theorists explain the new approach to women at work adopted by Asda and The Midland Bank? **[10]**

[AQA AS Specimen Paper – Unit 2 (Question 1)]

Examiner's tip

This question is one half of a module paper and so should take no more than 35 minutes to complete.

Answers

(1) (a)(i) Suggested Definition: The changing methods of working that require employees to accept greater variety in the way in which work is carried out. It may also mean less reliance on permanent full-time jobs.

(ii) Suggested Definition: Restructuring the organisation of a firm to increase efficiency. Usually done by reducing costs, especially overheads.

(b) • May lead to poor morale and motivation, which may reduce productivity.
- Reduced quality as a result of poorly motivated workers will damage sales and hence profit.
- Increased labour turnover will result from poor morale, which will increase workforce costs for the future, e.g. recruitment and training costs.
- Increased difficulty of recruiting workers of a high calibre if they know of the current problems.

(c) • Better workforce planning will increase the flexibility of the workforce.
- This will improve the firm's ability to forecast the supply and demand of labour.
- May need to change recruitment methods – to identify workers with more flexible skills.
- More training required of a more general nature to increase employees' flexibility and prepare them for the upcoming changes.

Examiner's tip

A question carrying this many marks will usually require you to question the difficulties of implementing your suggestions. How easy is it to identify future trends? Has the education system produced individuals with flexible skills? Will the costs of this forward-looking strategy be acceptable to the management of the firm?

(d) • Asda allowing 'shift swapping' tends to agree with Maslow's view that security is a factor – the responsibilities of women outside work are important.
- Flexible working at Midland Bank is recognising workers as human beings with other interests – Mayo.
- Herzberg explains the need to have motivators as well as maintenance factors – the provision of crèches or flexible working may act as a motivator.
- The majority of workers at Asda and Midland will be women. Therefore, both companies recognise that attracting and retaining female workers is very important. By offering more flexible arrangements for women they will be able to attract the best female workers and improve the service they provide to the customer.
- The real driving force may in fact be equal opportunities legislation, which managers will be more familiar with than motivational theorists. If they are seen to be ignoring these requirements they may attract unfavourable publicity, which is bad for business.

Examiner's tip

It is very important with questions about motivational theory that your answer does not become a repetition of all the theorists you can remember. You must apply the theory briefly to the case material.

Questions with model answers

C grade candidate – mark scored 15/30

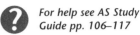 *For help see AS Study Guide pp. 106–117*

Valerie Fulton, of ntl, reveals how the Internet can draw a host of new admirers to your business.

How can I put my business on the Internet?
There are many talented web site designers available locally who will design your site for you. Prices range from around £50 per page. You then need to get the newly designed site onto the web and you can expect to pay at least £100 for set-up with a running cost of at least £50 per year.

How do I let people know about my new web site?
Many companies, including some of the best known in the world, have adapted their traditional newspaper and magazine advertising to direct customers to their web sites. All you have to do to promote your web site address is to add it to the bottom of adverts in the same way as you would use your phone number or mailing address. You can also add it to your stationery.

You have mentioned e-mail as a way of customers communicating with my business but I'd prefer to talk directly to anyone who has visited my web site. What's your advice?
The simplest solution is to provide a freephone number on your web site, that means that people who are interested will be able to phone you at no cost to themselves. Your web site and freephone number also have the advantage of allowing you to promote a 'national image' for your business even if you are working from a small office in a small town in Northern Ireland. One company I know of has had 2186 freephone calls as a result of its web site in just three months.

I'm tired of hearing about the need to put my business on the World Wide Web. What makes you think I need to do this?
The actual numbers of firms going onto the web and doing business is definitely growing. There are plenty of well-documented surveys from respected independent research companies. Anyone, anywhere in the world, can find out about your business. This is the marketing method of the future!

Source: adapted from The Business Telegraph 17 August, 1999 and 14 September, 1999

(a) Explain how a website and freephone number have the advantage of allowing a firm to promote a 'national image' even if it is run from a small office in a small town in Northern Ireland. **[6]**

(b) Discuss the impact that a new website may have on the traditional methods of promoting a business. **[10]**

(c) Evaluate the use of the Internet as a tool for mass marketing. **[14]**

[CCEA Specimen paper AS 3]

Examiner's Commentary

Questions with model answers

C grade candidate continued

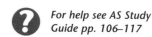

For help see AS Study Guide pp. 106–117

Examiner's Commentary

(a) A website will have its own 'www' address, which could be anywhere in the country ✔, and so it could easily be taken as a national company ✔. The offer of a freephone number is also associated with larger, nationally-based companies ✔.

(b) Businesses tend to use a combination of traditional advertising media such as TV, radio, newspapers and billboards, but this will depend on what is being sold and promoted. More and more people now have access to the Internet: as a result, businesses are creating their own websites to promote themselves and their products. This can be an efficient way of doing this, since it is low in cost ✔ and the website can be easy to maintain once it has been set up ✔. Some businesses now rely largely on their websites to sell their products or services, such as the 'dot.com' companies based on the Internet. They tend not to use the traditional methods of promotion ✔. Those businesses that do will have to reallocate some of their resources to Internet promotion ✔ ✔.

Although there are some well-explained points, the answer lacks detail, and some of it is not related fully to the question asked.

(c) I would recommend the use of an Internet website for any business. It brings a range of advantages, with hardly any drawbacks. Although there will be an initial cost in setting up the website ✔, the business will find that it will get many 'hits', perhaps even thousands, which will alert Internet users to the business and what it has to offer ✔ ✔. The advantages of the website are that it remains there even when the business premises are closed, so a customer can get in touch (using e-mail) at any time, day or night. This also allows the business to contact its customers through e-mail ✔ ✔. Since prospective customers in other countries can also find the business website ✔ ✔, sales are bound to increase.

An over-optimistic answer, which fails to analyse the limitations of websites. The answer would also be strengthened by comparing and contrasting with other tools for mass marketing.

A grade candidate – mark scored 27/30

(a) The information on the website will be under the control of the owners, and the firm's address need not feature ✔ ✔. There is also no way to tell where a firm is located from a freephone number ✔. The firm can therefore project a national image. The quality of the website and the way the freephone responses are handled are also factors in projecting an image ✔ ✔: a small firm can therefore create a professional image more associated with large companies ✔.

(b) The traditional methods of promoting products are being threatened through more frequent use of the Internet by people, as computers, mobile phones and other technological developments (e.g. TV shopping) lead towards greater Internet access ✔. One important factor is that, since there will be a limited budget for advertising and promotion, more and more of this budget may be being spent on the firm's website: as a result there will be less finance available for the more traditional promotional methods ✔ ✔. These

This is a good illustration of how to 'discuss', because a balanced answer has been presented.

A grade candidate continued

For help see AS Study Guide pp. 106–117

Examiner's Commentary

promotional methods will also be affected by the new website: for example, advertisements in papers and on radio will carry the firm's website address, encouraging people to access it ✔. More and more firms are using their websites not only to gain hits from potential customers, but also as a two-way medium, e.g. by allowing these customers to download catalogues, order forms, and other materials ✔. This can result in substantial cost savings for the firm (e.g. printing costs are borne by the customer, and less storage space is required by the firm) ✔.

The business can also promote its image and mission through its website. The 'virtual' business can be seen through pictures and video clips, and the image can be enhanced through professional presentation ✔. This compares well with the traditional methods of using brochures, and is very cost-effective when compared to the expense of corporate advertising through television or national newspapers ✔. The website must remain up-to-date, however, in order to promote a professional image.

The question asks about 'promoting a business', not just its products, which is recognised in this answer.

(c) Because the Internet is a global medium of communication, it has great value as a tool for mass marketing. Anyone with Internet access can access a firm's website from anywhere in the world ✔. It is also relatively inexpensive to establish an Internet presence ✔, and British firms are fortunate in that English is the dominant Internet language ✔. This is of tremendous benefit to many small firms that could only otherwise afford to promote on a small-scale (even local) basis ✔. The Internet site can be accessed 24 hours a day, every day, when the firm is otherwise 'closed'. It also lets a two-way dialogue take place: the company can allow access to materials such as downloadable brochures, and can set up ordering systems (e.g. using e-mail) ✔ ✔. In conclusion, the website compares favourably with many of the other, traditional, methods of mass promotion, on grounds of cost and accessibility ✔.

There is a clear analysis of the main issues of Internet use, although a clearer decision would strengthen the answer even further.

However, the website will need substantial promotion, especially in its early days ✔. Internet access in many countries is restricted, either by attempted government interference, or more commonly by the cost and availability of the required equipment ✔. Computer skills are also needed in order to access the Internet. Furthermore, it is not always easy, given the millions of pages available, for an individual firm to make its presence felt on the Internet ✔: it will need to rely on efficient searching by the user ✔, unless it can otherwise communicate its address (which will require the use of another medium, e.g. newspaper adverts featuring its website address). This searching is also likely to produce the websites of competitors, which may affect the firm's sales ✔. Finally, the Internet site will need to be regularly monitored and controlled, to ensure that it remains up-to-date and relevant for the firm's customers ✔, so there will be a continuing cost associated with its existence.

Exam practice questions

Answers on p. 43

(1) Read the following passage and then answer the questions that follow.

Boots Card tops ten million mark

Boots the Chemist will have ten million Advantage Cardholders by Christmas 1999, two million more than originally anticipated. The new figures also reveal that 95% of the cardholders are female.

The company claims the card has been successful because of its unique emotional positioning, which encourages customers to treat themselves to products using their loyalty points.

'The Advantage Card is our most important marketing tool and we have ambitious plans as to how we are going to use it next year,' said Crawford Davidson, Boots Advantage Card marketing group manager. This includes more segmented mailing according to lifestyle, level of loyalty and a prediction of types of products purchased, as well as changes to categories and store positioning.

Card data showed that new mothers buy more photographic material. Store planning and promotions around the traditionally male-interest category were given a more female focus.

(a) Explain **two** reasons why so many large retail businesses have introduced loyalty cards. **[4]**

(b) Discuss the view that the loyalty cards are ineffective unless all of the other necessary marketing elements are in place. **[6]**

(c) Analyse **both** the costs and benefits to Boots of placing greater emphasis on segmentation in its marketing policy. **[8]**

[WJEC Module 2 paper 2000]

Answers

(1) (a) • Loyalty cards allow segmentation to take place and provide Boots and other large retailers with information about their customers' shopping and buying habits.

   • As a result, such retailers can target their markets much more effectively.

   • The cards are a type of non-price competition: loyalty is created and repeat purchases encouraged, which benefits the retailer through retaining rather than losing the consumer.

Examiner's tip

Two reasons are asked for: at 2 marks per reason, make your points brief.

(b) The above answer suggests that the loyalty card can play an important role in overall marketing strategy.

   • It encourages repeat purchases, and provides the retailer with information that would otherwise not be available.

   • As a result, retailers can plan their marketing strategies more effectively.

   On its own, however, it is less effective than if it is used with other marketing ploys.

   • Examples from the marketing mix include promoting the card itself, and linking additional special offers with card purchases.

   • There must also be a satisfactory overall 'mix' for the card to be effective: e.g. suitable pricing policies, appropriate advertising and promotion, acceptable locations, and products that appeal to consumers.

   • The loyalty card will support this mix, but is of little use without it.

(c) 'Market segmentation' involves breaking the market into its constituent elements, e.g. on the basis of age, sex or other relevant characteristic.

   • An example is the existence of 'niche' markets, which appeal to and supply a single market segment.

   • As a result of segmentation, Boots can target different groups who have similar needs, and develop and promote products focused on these different groups.

   • Segmentation also encourages a policy of diversification, which is a safer policy for a firm than over-reliance on a single mass-market product.

   • One drawback of segmentation is that it may be more difficult to produce a standardised product for the mass market: the firm may therefore lose the opportunity of economies of scale.

   • However, mass market products will not appeal to everyone in the mass market, which is an argument in favour of segmentation policies.

Examiner's tip

It is often valuable to briefly define or describe a key term such as 'segmentation'.

Questions with model answers

C grade candidate – mark scored 6/14

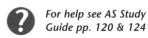
For help see AS Study Guide pp. 120 & 124

VERTIGO ROCK Ltd

Helen and Jenny Saunders have been running a small family company, making seaside rock and other confectionery novelties for the last 12 years. They have recently moved to a new industrial unit based in Eastbourne. The products they manufacture are traditional sticks of rock, in a range of different colours and flavours. This is fairly profitable, although the seasonal nature of the product does cause a number of production and financial problems.

The high demand in the summer months is not a problem, as they begin production soon after Christmas and build up stocks steadily. This is necessary as rock is best produced in small batches. The real problem is keeping their workers busy and funds coming in between October and March when not much rock is sold.

(a) Explain the meaning of batch production. **[4]**

(b) Helen has suggested that the company produce a range of Christmas rock novelties. Discuss the implications for production of this proposal. **[10]**

(a) The production of products in batches. The economic batch quantity can be calculated using a formula containing set-up costs, demand and holding costs ✔*.*

(b) The batch production method currently being used by Vertigo can be used for the production of Christmas rock novelties. They will probably be able to use the same machinery ✔*, although the workers may need extra training to teach them to make the new products* ✔*. This training may be on-the-job or off-the-job* ✔*. Vertigo will probably not be able to afford to provide much training so they will have to do it themselves* ✔*.*

The main problem with batch production is that time is lost having to change the equipment to produce different products. If they are now making different rock novelties they may find that their costs go up because they spend so much time resetting the equipment ✔*.*

Examiner's Commentary

This student has not defined the term. It is best to avoid using the word being defined in your definition. The answer gains one mark for evidence of some relevant knowledge about how the batch level can be calculated.

Although this student seems to know quite a bit about the method of production being used, the answer has two main faults. First, the sentences about the different types of training are not really relevant to the question and cannot therefore gain any marks. Second, there is poor use of the case material and so no real analysis can take place. Compare this with the answer by the student who gained an A grade.

A grade candidate – mark scored 13/14

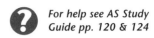

For help see AS Study Guide pp. 120 & 124

(a) This is when a limited number of products are made in one go, where the whole batch passes through one stage of production before moving on to the next ✔. This method is best used when the products are identical, except for one or two small changes ✔. For example, the sticks of rock are identical, except for the flavouring and colouring, which can be added to each batch as needed ✔.

(b) Helen's suggestion would help to fill the gap in the company's production run and provide very welcome extra finance ✔. However, there are a number of issues that they must consider before going ahead with the idea.

They need to be sure that there is a suitable market demand for the product and that the extra revenue gained will exceed the additional costs incurred ✔. Will new machinery be needed? ✔ Will the staff need retraining? ✔ The fact that they have just moved to new premises may mean there is sufficient space for expansion ✔, although it may also mean that they are still coming to terms with the new facilities and will not really want the added pressure caused by producing a new product ✔.

Ultimately, the fact that they have adequate spare capacity because of the seasonal nature of the rock ✔, and that the novelties are basically the same product should mean that any additional costs for machinery and training are minimal ✔. However, the potential benefits are great if it means that workers are kept busy ✔. Productivity is therefore improved and a more regular source of cash is achieved ✔.

Examiner's Commentary

The student has produced a clear definition and used the case material to provide an example.

A good answer needs to recognise that there are going to be some problems with any proposal.

Exam practice questions

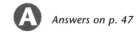

Answers on p. 47

(1) Barstow Engineering manufactures electrical motors sold to firms making washing machines and refrigerators. Production is organised into teams of workers each with a production supervisor. Any order is treated as a single batch and is allocated to a team, which is then responsible for its completion.

There has been heavy investment lately in production technology, thus creating flexibility and allowing teams to switch between products quickly. Since these changes, Barstow has become concerned about unreliable delivery of components by its supplier. Barstow's stock control chart for a particular component for the period January–May 1999 is shown in Figure 1. Quality control was not considered important, given the new machinery. Checking is now left to the supervisor. Labour turnover has increased over the past two years as the younger workers have left to join firms which offer training schemes. Recently, there have been a disturbing number of complaints about falling product standards and an increase in the number of rejected products returned by customers. One major customer has threatened to buy from a rival company if Barstow cannot produce a 'quality product'.

Figure 1
Stock control chart: component X

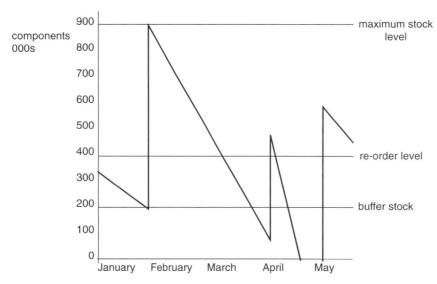

(a)(i) Explain and comment upon the term 'buffer stock' as used in Figure 1. **[4]**

(ii) Calculate the average monthly usage of component X. **[6]**

(iii) Define 'lead time' and calculate it for the April delivery of component X. **[4]**

(b) One supervisor has suggested that the investment in new production technology might have led to the recent complaints from customers. Discuss ways in which the situation might be improved. **[15]**

[OCR AS Specimen Paper – Business Decisions (Question 2)]

Examiner's tips

This question makes up one half of an AS module paper and therefore needs to be completed in no more than 35 minutes.

Answers

(1) (a) (i) • Barstow Engineering have a buffer stock level of 200 000 units.
  • They intend to ensure that they never let the stock of this particular component fall below 200 000.
  • To prevent the problems associated with running out of stocks.

Examiner's tip

To show a good understanding of the case material you could mention that the level chosen needs to be reassessed given the stockout that occurred at the end of April.

(ii) Total Purchased =

$$
\begin{array}{r}
700\ 000 \\
400\ 000 \\
600\ 000\ + \\
\hline
1\ 700\ 000
\end{array}
$$

Examiner's tips

The three figures are found by calculating the size of orders in February, April and May.

Stock Level Increase = Opening Stock – Closing Stock

$$
\begin{array}{r}
=\quad 450\ 000 \\
350\ 000\ - \\
\hline
=\quad 100\ 000
\end{array}
$$

Examiner's tips

It is always a good idea to show as many stages of the working as possible. This helps you to work logically and helps the examiner to see how you got to the answer.

Total Sales

$$
\begin{array}{r}
=\ 1\ 700\ 000 \\
100,000\ - \\
\hline
=\ 1\ 600\ 000
\end{array}
$$

Average Monthly Sales = 1 600 000/5 = 320 000

(iii) The lead time is the time taken between re-ordering the component from the supplier and the time when the new stock is received.

The stock received in April was ordered in March, so the lead time is one month.

Examiner's tip

The lead time can be easily identified by following the stock level line back from the month when the stock arrives to the point where the line passes through the re-order level indicated by the horizontal line.

(b) • Process will have become more mechanised – especially the use of CAM.
  • May demotivate workers, especially if they see colleagues being made redundant.
  • Removes opportunities for promotion.
  • Introduce better training or a strategy of TQM.
  • Introduce quality assurance rather than quality control to involve all the workers.
  • Will empower the workers and should be easy to implement as they already work in teams.
  • Ask customers for feedback to help identify the cause of the problem.
  • May be other causes of the problem, such as switching of team members, high labour turnover and an unreliable supplier.

Examiner's tips

You need to combine knowledge of relevant theory with the information given about Barstow Engineering. It is helpful to first identify the problems. The solutions can then be clearly linked to the problems identified.

Questions with model answers

C grade candidate – mark scored 10/20

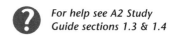

For help see A2 Study Guide sections 1.3 & 1.4

CHARITIES: WHEN BIG BUSINESS PLAYS ITS PART GIVING MONEY ISN'T THE ONLY WAY TO HELP by Ellen Davies

Are donations simply made for selfish reasons, to buy reputation? Some companies deny that their motives are anything but altruistic – but, says Peter Hunt, community programme manager for Shell UK, giving money to good causes for purely philanthropic reasons is unethical: 'The money belongs to our shareholders and we have to make it grow. I have a moral problem with giving money away without any benefit to the business.' Shell's total contribution to charity in the UK last year was about £5.5 million, and only £1.8 million of that was cash.

'Giving money is often the least effective way of helping,' Hunt argues. 'It's like pouring water into the desert.'

Shell prefers to work with charities to build long-term programmes, looking at areas where there are business links – education, enterprise and the environment: 'We look for the people who are doing good work and pushing things forward, where we can contribute something significant.'

Source: adapted from *The Daily Telegraph*, 14 December, 1995

ANITA AND GORDON RODDICK LAUNCHING AN ADVERTISEMENT

Anita and Gordon Roddick are breaking with one of Body Shop's longest-held traditions by launching an advertisement on Monday. The advert, though, will not be promoting Body Shop, but a Channel 4 documentary due to be screened that evening, called *The Drilling Fields*.

It concerns Shell's exploration activities in Nigeria and the opposition to them from the Ogoni tribe, whose tribal lands are affected. Roddick and the programme makers claim 1 000 people have died in clashes between the Ogoni and government forces protecting Shell representatives.

Source: The Daily Telegraph, 21 May, 1994

(a) Analyse the possible effects for Body Shop of their concern for ethical issues. **[8]**

(b) With reference to *both* articles, evaluate whether businesses are becoming more ethically and socially responsible. **[12]**

Examiner's Commentary

C grade candidate continued

For help see A2 Study Guide sections 1.3 & 1.4

(a) Body Shop will be able to sell more of its products because at the moment it is very popular to be ethically and environmentally friendly. People who dislike Shell's treatment of the Ogoni tribe will feel more positive towards Body Shop and so buy more of its products. Body Shop will gain good publicity from this venture and this explains why it does not have to spend as much on advertising and marketing as other competitors ✔. It is able to rely far more on the brand loyalty of its customers ✔. The people who are not bothered about Shell's treatment of the Ogoni will probably not be likely to buy from Body Shop in any case.

Another effect of Body Shop being interested in ethical matters is that it will be able to attract better-quality ✔ and more committed employees ✔. People will like working for Body Shop and will be less likely to leave.

(b) In donating over £5 million to charity it is clear that Shell is trying to be more socially responsible. It knows that as a company it is seen as damaging to the environment, both because of petrol pollution ✔ and bad publicity surrounding the dumping of disused oil platforms at sea ✔. It will be making these donations to help raise the public's opinion of it as a company ✔.

However, it is likely that many potential customers of Shell will not be aware of its promotion of good causes and will not see it as being ethical ✔.

The fact that their community programme manager clearly states that they are only making donations to charity where it makes business sense suggests that Shell is not being ethical at all and is rather doing it for the wrong reasons ✔.

Body Shop has always been a company with high ethical standards and its involvement with the publicity surrounding the Ogoni tribe does not provide any evidence that business is becoming more ethical ✔.

Examiner's Commentary

This is an interesting point, but it is a shame it has not been explained.

Although it does not state so explicitly in the question, if you are asked for the effects of something happening you should always look to provide a balanced argument to gain more than half marks.

It is a shame that this point was not developed.

This answer suffers for two reasons. First, it does not really answer the question set. It generally explains the potential reasons for Shell's strategy for giving to charity, but does not analyse whether this means they are becoming more ethical. Second, it is primarily about Shell, and only mentions Body Shop as an afterthought. There should be a more balanced coverage of the two articles.

Questions with model answers

A grade candidate – mark scored 20/20

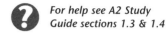
For help see A2 Study Guide sections 1.3 & 1.4

Examiner's Commentary

(a) By showing a concern for ethical issues Body Shop may expect to maintain or improve their reputation and retain the customer's positive view of the company ✔. Body Shop has relied on this brand loyalty from its customers in recent years as it has fought to compete against larger, more powerful competitors ✔. It can be argued that it has been able to attract customers because of its ethical stance. Ethical concern may also attract better, more motivated staff ✔, at a time when it is becoming increasingly difficult to recruit and retain good quality staff because of low unemployment. Recruiting staff who are sympathetic to Body Shop's ethical standpoint will mean that staff turnover, absenteeism, loyalty and ultimately productivity will be improved ✔ ✔.

> *This shows an awareness of current external factors.*

However, it must also be recognised that ethical practices may act as a constraint. Body Shop's attitude towards animal testing at a time when this was common practice will have increased its costs. The time taken to research potential suppliers to ensure that they conform to Body Shop's ethical standards will have proven costly and ultimately may have denied it many suppliers ✔. Even when a supplier is chosen, time and money will have to be spent to monitor continuously whether the supplier is keeping to the code of conduct required ✔.

Body Shop may alienate many customers who are loyal to Shell, and believe that what they are doing in Nigeria is not wrong. The amount of time that Body Shop spend on promoting ethical issues of concern may mean that other aspects of managing the company are ignored or poorly carried out ✔.

> *The word 'analyse' in the question indicates that the pros and cons need to be covered with some discussion but certainly no attempt to evaluate is required.*

(b) There is some evidence in the articles to support both sides of the argument about whether companies are becoming more ethical. Shell donated £5.5 million during 1995. This may indicate that they have a desire to see disadvantaged groups in society benefit ✔. However, when one considers the size of this donation against the likely size of Shell's profits it may be seen as too little ✔.

> *Good to see that the writer of this answer does not take evidence solely at face value.*

It is an interesting argument put forward by Peter Hunt. He is suggesting that actually making large contributions to charity is in itself unethical. This is of course seen from the point of view of shareholders, whose profits are their rewards from investing in Shell ✔. Dividends are seen to be the payback for shareholders' risk taking. It may be argued that investing in such a large and financially successful company as Shell does not in fact possess much risk and dividends do not need to be so high ✔. Peter Hunt is disregarding other stakeholders' views on this topic and suggests that Shell see their shareholders as being the most important stakeholder: not necessarily a very ethical approach to business ✔.

A grade candidate continued

For help see A2 Study Guide sections 1.3 & 1.4

Examiner's Commentary

The comment about not 'giving money away without any benefit to the business' may indicate the true attitude to charitable donations by Shell. This statement suggests that they see it as a marketing exercise and they will only donate if the returns to Shell are greater than the cost ✔. This may be regarded as an unethical attitude and indicative of most large companies' approach to donations. It would appear that Shell's contributions to charity come out of their marketing rather than their charitable donations budget ✔.

Comparison of costs and benefits will usually be seen as evaluation.

In contrast to this, Body Shop has taken time and effort to promote a campaign about an issue directly unrelated to its line of business. Any campaign against Shell cannot be regarded as being part of marketing, as Shell and Body Shop have completely unrelated lines of business ✔. Body Shop has spent its own money on producing the advertisement which is not promoting its product, although the cynical attitude may be that it is still good promotion ✔.

A good answer will always identify opposite points of view.

In conclusion, it is very difficult to conclude whether companies are becoming more ethical or not. The information provided in the two articles is very limited and there is no way to allow a comparison with previous years ✔. Also, the information gives a mixed picture about the behaviour of business. On the one hand, Body Shop has always maintained a very high profile concerning matters of ethical and socially responsible behaviour ✔. On the other hand, Shell and the oil industry in general, have had to react to considerable bad publicity about the safety of oil platforms, the dumping of these in the North Sea and the long-term costs of pollution from fossil fuels ✔.

Another acceptable way to evaluate. The lack of suitable evidence to make a balanced judgement.

Exam practice questions

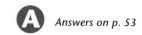 *Answers on p. 53*

(1)   **A TIGHTENING LABOUR MARKET**

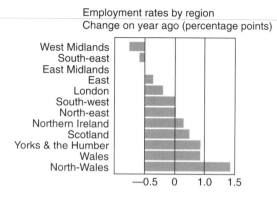
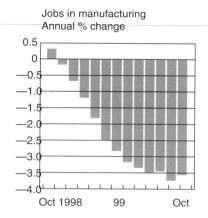

Sources: ONS; Primark Datastream

Growing bonuses are helping to push up pay increases, fuelling expectations that the Bank of England may soon need to raise interest rates again. October alone saw average earnings growth speed up to 5.1% compared to 4.6% in September. Much of the increase is due to increased bonus payments in real estate, business services, the retail sector and the banking and financial services sectors.

The Bank may also be concerned at signs of tightening in the labour market, with another fall in unemployment. The number of people in work rose by an estimated 66 000 between August and October and this means that nearly 27.5 million people are in paid employment. Andrew Oswald, Professor of Economics at Warwick University, warns that inflation may soon be a problem and that, 'a tightening labour market and rising oil prices could spell trouble for the economy by the middle of next year'.

Source: Adapted from *The Financial Times*, 16 December, 1999

(a)   Briefly explain the meaning of the following:
　(i)   inflation
　(ii)   a tightening labour market.   **[4]**

(b)   Explain why rising average earnings may or may not contribute to inflationary pressure in the United Kingdom economy.   **[6]**

(c)   Discuss the arguments for and against the raising of interest rates, by the Bank of England, as a means of solving the inflationary problems indicated in the passage.   **[8]**

[WJEC June 2000 – Module 4 (Question 1)]

Answers

(1) (a) (i) Suggested definition: A sustained increase in the average price of products in an economy over a period of time.

(ii) Suggested definition: When unemployment is falling and it is therefore more difficult to recruit employees. It usually leads to wages being forced up because of excess demand for labour.

(b) Rising wages may lead to Demand-Pull Inflation. Increased spending may exceed the required increases in supply, especially if labour supply is limited.

Rising labour costs which, if not matched by improved productivity, will work through to cause price rises and hence Cost-Push Inflation

However, this assumes that wage rises automatically lead to increased demand and higher costs. Higher taxes or more saving may account for some or all of the higher wage. Also, firms making reasonable profits may be able to absorb an increase in labour costs by reducing profits.

Examiner's tip

The ability to develop your argument about the links between rising wages and inflation is vital for top marks.

(c) Arguments in favour of raising interest rates include:
- They discourage spending and encourage saving.
- They may strengthen sterling's exchange rate so that imported raw materials are cheaper and economic growth slows down, both of which will help control inflation.
- Increased interest costs for firms may encourage them to look for improved efficiencies elsewhere.

However, there are a number of good arguments against the use of interest rates:
- Firms may pass higher interest costs onto their customers in the form of higher prices.
- May create unemployment in the longer term because of falling aggregate demand.
- It is difficult to predict the exact size and timing of the impact of higher interest rates.
- Nowadays there is less of a link between higher interest rates and reduced post-mortgage income because of the increased availability and popularity of fixed interest rate deals.

Examiner's tip

To gain top marks you need to be able to recognise the wider implications of a rise in interest rates. You may also briefly refer to other means of solving inflationary pressure, including supply-side policies and fiscal policy.

Questions with model answers

C grade candidate – mark scored 11/22

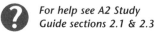

*For help see A2 Study
Guide sections 2.1 & 2.3*

WHITBREAD SELLS ALL 3 000 PUBS

Examiner's Commentary

Whitbread heralded the end of an era yesterday when the former brewing giant put its 3 000-strong pub estate up for sale to concentrate on leisure activities.

The sale of the pub estate, which is estimated to be worth £1.5 billion, comes hard on the heels of the £400m disposal of Whitbread's brewing activities to Interbrew.

The sale will leave Whitbread to concentrate on its hotel brands Marriott and Travel Inn, restaurant brands Beefeater, Bella Pasta and Café Rouge and the David Lloyd leisure business.

'We are selling a business that is outperforming its marketplace with a management with a high reputation', Sir John Banham, the chairman, said yesterday. 'This is just a continuation of our strategy to reduce dependence on beer.' He said that two-thirds of the money derived from the sale of the pub estate would be distributed among shareholders. This would amount to around £2 a share. Whitbread shares shot up $37\frac{1}{2}$p to 469p at the news.

Sir John said the company was working to improve lacklustre brands such as Beefeater, by rebranding most of its 258 restaurants, with about 80 becoming a new concept, Out and Out, aimed at middle-class diners. The whole group had to achieve like-for-like sales growth of 5%, which would produce 'double digit profits growth'. Over the last half year, hotels' underlying sales rose by 9.8%, with operating profits up 85% to £46m. Restaurants' comparable sales were up 2.2% with operating profits up 8.2% to £65.7m. Fitness club profits rose 26% to £13.1m.

Source: adapted from *The Daily Telegraph*, 20 October & 1 November, 2000

(a)   Discuss the possible reasons why Whitbread decided to sell off its brewing activities to Interbrew.   **[10]**

(b)   Evaluate how the strategy of rebranding the Beefeater restaurants will affect Whitbread's stakeholders.   **[12]**

(a) Whitbread may have sold their brewing activities for a number of reasons. They may have needed the money gained from selling this part of the business ✔. *£400 million is a lot of money and it may have allowed them to do other things. We are told in the passage that the hotel part of the company has grown by 9.8%. This fast-growing sector is also producing very high profits* ✔. *If more money is invested in these two sectors Whitbread may benefit to a greater extent than they currently do in the brewing industry* ✔.

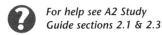

For help see A2 Study Guide sections 2.1 & 2.3

C grade candidate continued

Brewing may have been uncompetitive and unprofitable. Selling the brewery will mean that another specialist firm such as Interbrew can try to make the business more efficient and eventually profitable ✔. It may be the case that Whitbread have diversified too much and this has meant that they are unable to spend enough time building up the brewing side of the business ✔. Alternatively, they may find that their managers are now more geared up to other sectors of the leisure industry, especially as they have now announced that they are to sell their pub estate ✔, and do not have the knowledge and skill to turn the brewery around financially ✔.

(b) Stakeholders are those individuals or groups with a direct interest in a company's actions. I am going to examine the effect on employees, banks, customers and the community.

The employees may be affected because the new restaurant will employ better quality workers. This will mean that the present staff are made redundant.

The banks may be concerned because the rebranding will cost money that Whitbread may have to borrow ✔. Also, if the new restaurants are not successful, this may affect the company's ability to repay interest on other loans they may have ✔.

Customers will benefit because they will get a new type of restaurant ✔. They will have more choice, although the prices will be higher.

The local community may suffer because some workers will now be out of work, although some others will have gained jobs ✔.

Examiner's Commentary

This answer, although only dealing with a couple of possible reasons does try to explain the reasoning. It gains more than half marks because it uses some evidence from the article to analyse what may have happened.

Are these two restaurants going to be so different that some or all of the staff cannot be retrained?

What about the fact that the new brand is really being aimed at a different market segment?

A grade candidate – mark scored 21/22

(a) It may appear surprising that Whitbread has decided to sell off its brewing activities when we are told that the business is `outperforming its marketplace with a management with a high reputation´. If this sector of the business is doing so well then we must assume that Whitbread has good reason to sell up. First, although we are told that it is performing well and has good management, we are not told whether the brewing sector is profitable ✔. In recent years this industry has seen a lot of competition with many large brewers merging. It may well be that the brewing industry is not particularly profitable and, although Whitbread are doing well, this is still not as good as in the other sectors of their business ✔.

Questions with model answers

A grade candidate continued

 For help see A2 Study Guide sections 2.1 & 2.3

Examiner's Commentary

Second, if Whitbread had a long-term strategy of selling their pubs, which they have now announced, the sale of the brewing sector may have been decided as a logical part of this overall strategy ✔. Without pubs to sell their beer, it may have been considered too difficult and expensive to find suitable distribution channels ✔.

Good incorporation of issues learnt in the AS part of the course.

Third, we are told that the sale of the brewing sector has raised £400 million. This is a sizeable amount of finance to allow the expansion into other more profitable sectors of the leisure industry. The large and growing revenue and profit figures quoted for these sectors will make further investment in them very attractive ✔. There is a danger that if Whitbread do not carry out the necessary investment now they will be left behind. This level of investment may not be possible with more traditional sources of finance, such as borrowing ✔. (Whitbread may in fact be unable to raise any more finance via banks or shareholders.)

It is good to see an answer that does not assume facts that are unknown, but raises the issues that may apply.

Finally, the decision to 'reduce dependence on beer' suggests that Whitbread recognise that they should not rely on this sector in the future ✔. In today's market it is dangerous to rely on one particular product, especially if that product is not highly profitable.

In conclusion, it is clear that Whitbread have sold their brewing interests as part of a clear long-term strategy. It has raised finance for expansion in more profitable markets and has allowed them to have a more diverse portfolio of products ✔. It may well be that Whitbread saw Interbrew as a company who could take over their brewing activities and because of their specialisation be more efficient at it, so making greater profits ✔. In this case, Whitbread may have been able to receive a price for the brewing assets greater than their value on the Whitbread balance sheet.

This is a good conclusion. It does not just repeat points made earlier. There is a good attempt to put together the main issues.

(b) When considering the impact on different stakeholders the main issue is that each of them has different objectives. Whitbread must balance these objectives to ensure that all stakeholders are happy and that conflict is minimised.

This is an excellent start, which immediately highlights the potential conflict of objectives.

One of the main groups of stakeholders are Whitbread's shareholders. They will expect a good return from their investment in the form of dividends and an increase in the share price. By rebranding some of the Beefeater restaurants Whitbread are aiming to increase their appeal, especially amongst middle-class diners ✔. These diners will have more disposable income and so will expect a different quality of service than that currently offered. This may mean that prices can be higher, although this will not automatically mean more profit, as costs will presumably also be higher ✔.

Questions with model answers

A grade candidate continued

For help see A2 Study Guide sections 2.1 & 2.3

Examiner's Commentary

In fact, the extra costs in the short run of carrying out a rebranding strategy may mean that any benefits will be in the long run. Therefore, shareholders may see a fall in their dividend and share price initially ✔. Growth in the restaurant sector appears slow at the moment compared to the other sectors in which Whitbread are involved ✔. From the shareholders´ viewpoint they might have preferred to see current marketing efforts in the faster growing hotel or fitness club sectors ✔.

The customer is another important stakeholder. The switch in target market will mean that some customers will find that their local Beefeater restaurant will now be rebranded and possibly be outside their price-bracket ✔. These customers will feel neglected and may desert other Whitbread-owned companies ✔. The new `Out and Out´ restaurants will be targeted at new customers who may become vital assets to all of Whitbread´s companies. Whitbread may feel that the new restaurant brand will better attract the type of customer currently loyal to Whitbread in their fitness clubs and hotels.

Suppliers will also be affected as some raw materials and components used in the new restaurants will be different from before ✔. Better quality food, a higher standard of furniture and different advertising channels may mean that some suppliers are replaced ✔.

The employees may also be greatly affected. To provide a higher level of service the chefs and waiting-on staff may need to be retrained ✔. This may however be viewed as an advantage for them, as it will increase their skills and qualifications, as well as making them more employable in the future. They may also see their wages being increased ✔.

It is clear to see that all stakeholders will be affected by the proposed change in different ways. Ultimately, the magnitude of the effect will vary, depending on how successful this rebranding exercise is. If it is successful and increases profits in the long run, shareholders, customers and employees will clearly benefit. It may also mean that more of the Beefeater restaurants are rebranded. If, however, the strategy is a failure, employees may lose their jobs, shareholders will see smaller dividends and customers will regard Whitbread as a failure ✔.

> *Any attempt to assess long-run versus short-run issues will be rewarded highly.*

> *The topic of stakeholders is one that occurs throughout the course. Notice how when it is dealt with in the A2 part of the course it is much more integrated with other issues, such as Marketing and Human Resources.*

Exam practice questions

Answers on p. 59

OLIGOPOLY – BAD NEWS FOR HOLIDAYMAKERS?

(1) The outlook for the small holiday firms and holidaymakers is looking as gloomy as an English summer at the moment.

The first problem is whether the results of recent mergers and takeovers are going to lead to higher prices and less choice for consumers. More than two-thirds of overseas holidays are in the hands of Thomson, Airtours, Thomas Cook and First Choice. The recent merger of Thomas Cook and Carlson now means this group owns one in five of all travel agencies, operating nearly 1400 agencies in the UK. Of 21 million holidays on sale in June 1998 the 'big four' accounted for 14.2 million. The small independent agents, such as the 156 members of the Association of Independent Tour Operators (AITO), expect to sell only 2 million holidays between them, about half that of the Thomson group. The independents fear they will be squeezed out of hotels and airlines by the superior buying power of their dominant rivals and that competition and consumer choice will suffer. It is not only in the ownership of agencies and holidays that the small firms feel threatened. Charter airlines such as Britannia Airways, Air 2000, Airtours International and Caledonian are also in the hands of the 'big four'. AITO has now written to the Office of Fair Trading urging government action to prevent further concentration of ownership.

At the same time the industry is having to cope with the effects of increasing fuel taxes, departure tax, changes in interest rates and fluctuations in exchange rates set against a background of statistics that suggest the economy is going into recession.

Source: Adapted from *The Times Weekend*, Saturday 10 October, 1998
by Tom Chesshyre and Jannette Hyde

(a) Explain why the 'big four' may seek to avoid reducing prices to customers. **[2]**

(b) Evaluate mergers and takeovers as a strategy for growth. **[8]**

(c) How would you account for the continued survival and success of so many small agents in the holiday industry? **[6]**

[Edexcel A Level, June 2000 – Paper 2 (Question B3 a–c)]

Answers

(1) (a) Because the firms are interdependent and Oligopoly-like in structure they need to avoid a price war. Price stability is important for everyone's survival.

(b) Mergers and takeovers may be an attractive option for growth because the alternative, organic growth, is very slow. By joining with another company you are provided with a ready-made market. It also reduces competition, provides expertise in new areas and with an established company is less risky.

However, if a company does not do sufficient research it may find that the company being taken over or merged with is inefficient or unsuitable. There is a danger of over-expansion and the Competition Commission may object or place restrictions on the deal.

Examiner's tip

Evaluation requires you to weigh up the arguments from each side.

(c) The smaller travel firm may be catering for niche markets, e.g. coach holidays, holidays for walkers, etc. The specialisation they can practise will provide for a more personalised service. There are limited opportunities for economies of scale in the industry because of the labour intensity. There are very few start-up costs and therefore few barriers to entry.

Questions with model answers

C grade candidate – mark scored 10/20

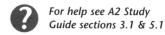
For help see A2 Study Guide sections 3.1 & 5.1

(a)   How useful is the Boston Matrix in helping businesses analyse their product portfolio?   **[8]**

(b)   'According to the theory of the Boston Matrix single product firms are unlikely to be successful in the long run.'
Evaluate this statement.   **[12]**

[WJEC Specimen paper BS4]

Examiner's Commentary

(a) The Boston Matrix or 'Boston Box' sets out to analyse a company's products under four headings: cash cows, stars, dogs, problem children ✔.

> *A good start, but the candidate then fails to explain either the purpose of the Matrix or its constituent elements.*

The Boston Matrix shows visually where the firm stands with its products ✔. Lots of 'dogs' means it should probably drop these products as soon as possible so that it can use the resources elsewhere. Lots of 'stars' means it must make sure they are kept and developed, to turn into 'cash cows' ✔.

The Matrix doesn't take everything into account: for example, competitor actions ✔. It won't therefore answer all the firm's questions to do with the range of products it sells.

> *The candidate makes a relevant point regarding the limitations of the Matrix, but then doesn't follow this up. You won't score many marks for a limited explanation and analysis such as this.*

(b) A single-product firm is just that: it makes and sells a single product. It may be doing this successfully - for example, in a niche market. A 'niche market' is one where the firm concentrates on just one market segment ✔ ✔. Although this can be profitable, the firm is taking a lot of risks ✔. For example, the niche market may collapse due to the actions of a government or a competitor, and people simply change tastes or fashion ✔ ✔. If the firm relies on a single product, it will become bankrupt.

> *The candidate has described satisfactorily the difficulties that a single-product firm may find itself in, but has not provided any reasonable explanation of how the single-product firm can use the Matrix to analyse its product.*

The Boston Box is designed for firms with more than one product ✔, so it is of no real use to the single-product firm.

A grade candidate – mark scored 19/20

(a) The Boston Matrix is a product portfolio analysis technique. It analyses products under four headings, showing the market share of each product and the rate of growth for the markets in which they are sold ✔. This is the appearance of the 'Box' ✔.

A grade candidate continued

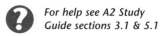

For help see A2 Study Guide sections 3.1 & 5.1

Examiner's Commentary

`Stars´ are potentially highly profitable products, and heavy investment should convert them into `cash cows´, the key to the firm´s profits and sales. `Problem children´ are also known as `question marks´, and serve the purpose of plugging a hole in the firm´s product range. `Dogs´ are the unprofitable products that are also major users of the firm´s resources ✔ ✔.

Once the firm´s product portfolio has been analysed using the Matrix, the marketing department can decide on its marketing strategies. If, for example, most products have been classified as `cash cows´, this suggests that the firm needs to start concentrating on new product development to maintain growth in the future ✔. The limitations of the Matrix are, first, that it remains only a planning tool and will not decide the firm´s marketing strategy on its own ✔; second, placing products under the various headings can sometimes be difficult (e.g. as a result of limited market information) ✔; third, there are many relevant features of a product that are not taken into account by the Matrix ✔.

The answer contains a diagram and explanation of the contents of the 'Box': this is a good idea so long as it doesn't dominate the answer, and it is supported by analysis and evaluation, as is the case here.

(b) The main benefit of using the Boston Matrix is that it encourages firms to examine the breadth of their product portfolio. It therefore most obviously relates to a large multi-product firm having a substantial product portfolio ✔ ✔. The Matrix may still be useful to a single-product firm, however. The well-known problem that any single-product firm faces is having `all its eggs in one basket´ ✔: if there is a major change in market demand, e.g. due to some innovation or technological development by a competitor, the single-product firm can find it difficult to respond ✔ ✔.

But a single-product firm may still have `different´ products. If only one product is being manufactured by a firm, it may still feature in more than one part of the `Box´ ✔: for example, if the firm exports the product as well as selling it in the UK. In the UK market, for example, it may be a `cash cow´, whereas in another market such as Germany, it could be a `star´ ✔. Product differentiation can also exist in the same market, e.g. through the firm adopting differentiated pricing policies or otherwise concentrating on a unique selling point of the product with one segment of its market ✔ ✔. Some firms actively pursue, and are content with, a niche marketing position, making a single product and surviving profitably in this niche market ✔.

This is related well to the case study situation.

The Boston Matrix still has a role to play for a single-product firm, and the firm may well survive in the long run if it is able to differentiate its product in some way, or use market segmentation effectively ✔.

There is an assumption that a single product appears in just one section of the Matrix: this answer points out that this may not necessarily be so.

Exam practice questions

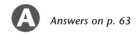 *Answers on p. 63*

(1) Chocalot Ltd is a manufacturer of a small but expensive range of chocolate confectionery. Sales in recent years have varied considerably. The peak sales period is usually the run-up to Christmas and sales are at their lowest during the summer months. The directors are planning to expand the company's capacity and have already attempted to increase sales at other times of the year. They are anxious to establish the seasonal variation in sales and to forecast future sales levels. The following data relates to sales in recent years:

Year	Quarter	Sales (£000)	4 quarter moving average
1997	3	130	
	4	128	
			132.75
1998	1	118	
			131.50
	2	155	
			134.50
	3	125	
			138.00
	4	140	
			136.75
1999	1	132	
			137.25
	2	150	
			137.25
	3	127	
			134.25
	4	140	
2000	1	120	

(a) Using the four quarter moving average calculation given, centre the results using an appropriate method on the insert provided and from this show the predicted trend value for sales for quarter 2 in 2000. **[8]**

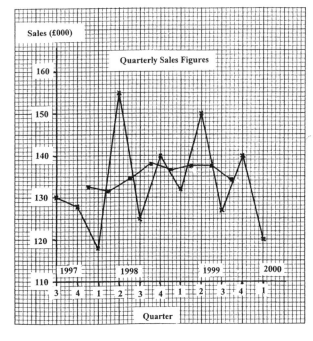

(b) Using your results, calculate the average seasonal variation for the second quarter. **[4]**

(c) In the light of your results, assess the company's intentions to raise its capacity and to try to increase sales. **[5]**

(d) Evaluate the appropriateness of time-series analysis as a method of forecasting sales for a business operating in a luxury product market. **[8]**

[Total 25 marks]

[Edexcel 2000 paper 2]

Answers

(a)

1997	3		
	4		
		132.75	
1998	1		132.125
		131.50	
	2		133.00
		134.50	
	3		136.25
		138.00	
	4		137.375
		136.75	
1999	1		137.00
		137.25	
	2		137.25
		137.25	
	3		135.75
		134.25	
	4		
2000	1		

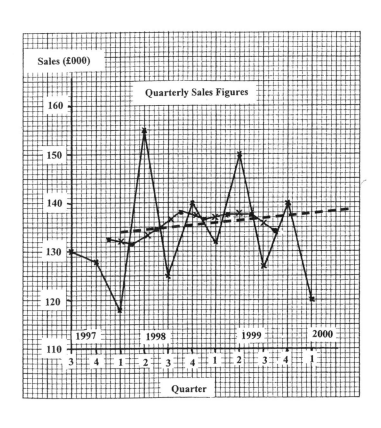

(b) • Average seasonal variation for quarter 2 is:
(1998) Actual 155 less 133 = + 22
(1999) Actual 150 less 137.25 = + 12.75
• Overall average = (+ 22 and + 12.75 divided by 2) + 17.375

(c) The trend suggests that there is no dramatic increase, and capacity already seems to exist judging by the sales figures. The company may be better advised to try evening its sales out to a greater extent.

(d) • In general, time-series analysis depends on the reliability of the data used, provides a purely quantitative analysis, and also ignores random external variations (the unpredictable element).
• It is only really of use in the short term, and is based on the assumption that history repeats itself: the evidence Chocalot Ltd has suggests this doesn't happen in its market, since there is a reference that: 'Sales in recent years have varied considerably.'
• Time-series may be better suited to a mass market analysis, since the luxury chocolate market may not provide adequate or suitable data for analysis, and may also be subject to major unpredictable occurrences (e.g. health scares for chocolate).

Examiner's tip

Comments on the general strengths and weaknesses of time-series analysis have to be tailored to the nature of a luxury market.

Questions with model answers

C grade candidate – mark scored 16/30

For help see A2 Study Guide sections 4.1 & 4.2

McVeigh Engineering Ltd, a medium-sized family business, is concerned about the quantity and quality of information received by its managers at all levels. Its senior management team met last week to discuss the situation. The Managing Director was very worried by this discussion. It was reported at the meeting that the business had been disadvantaged because managers hadn't been given the appropriate information. As a result, the firm has decided to introduce a Management Information System which will be based around increased use of computer technology. All offices will be networked with up-to-date computer equipment and managers will have their own computer terminals on their desks.

(a) What is the purpose of a Management Information System? **[8]**

(b) Examine the issues which would have to be considered when designing an effective Management Information System for McVeigh Engineering Ltd. **[10]**

(c) Evaluate the impact on McVeigh Engineering Ltd of networking all its offices with up-to-date computer equipment and giving managers their own computer terminals on their desks. **[12]**

[CCEA 2000 Paper 1]

Examiner's Commentary

(a) Management needs information in order to help the firm survive. The management information system will provide this information so that managers can carry out their job of planning and controlling ✔ ✔. Information from the management information system will therefore enable the firm to meets its stated objectives (e.g. market growth, increased profit) ✔ ✔.

(b) With any new system, a business has to consider three main areas. First, its cost. The cost must be affordable to the business, otherwise the system will cost more than the value of the information it is giving to the management ✔ ✔. Second, the people. The family here may have their own views about the type of system to be designed, and the designers will need to talk to them about this system ✔. Not only the family, but also all staff, some of whom will need a different sort of information, notably more detailed information to help them with their day-to-day work ✔. Third, the structure of the business. A function-based business will have a hierarchy through which the information needs to pass. Designers will need to analyse this hierarchy, e.g. checking formal and informal lines of communication, in order to design an effective system ✔.

(c) The positive side of the new system will be the speed and accuracy of what is produced, which seems to be needed by this business ✔. It is likely that

> The candidate should have started by clarifying the term used: this provides a focus for answering the question.

> Although the candidate has made three points, this answer is very general. There is little analysis of the case-study information, and limited reference only to the company.

C grade candidate continued

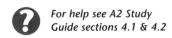 For help see A2 Study
Guide sections 4.1 & 4.2

Examiner's Commentary

there will be an e-mail network within the business: this is quick and efficient, although sometimes it can be abused ✔. The network may also have Internet access, which will enable managers to get a lot of information from outside the business. This is particularly helpful for managers in, say, marketing, where the information could be used for forecasting ✔ ✔.

The downside of the system will obviously be its cost (see (b) above). Managers will need training in the use of this equipment, and it may be that some of them will resent having to use computers ✔ ✔. Also, `GIGO´ - garbage in, garbage out - is associated with a computer-based information system ✔.

> There is no conclusion. Marks are often awarded for a conclusion where the candidate makes a judgement: here, no judgement has been made.

A grade candidate – mark scored 28/30

(a) The main roles of managers are to take decisions, and to plan, co-ordinate and control their firm ✔. Information is needed by managers and other staff for these purposes ✔, but this information normally first arrives in the firm in the form of unstructured data ✔. Examples include information from various sources about the firm´s sales, paperwork to do with buying (e.g. invoices, orders), production figures, and so on ✔. A management information system (MIS) sets out to change the data the firm has received into meaningful information ✔. The MIS then uses a suitable format (e.g. number, text or diagrams; electronic or paper) to transmit this information to managers and others requiring it ✔ ✔. The key purpose of MIS is therefore to provide information for decision-making.

> To save valuable writing time, using a well-known and popular abbreviation like 'MIS' is acceptable, but still include in your answer at least one reference to the full description.

(b) What we are told about the firm is that McVeigh Engineering Ltd is a medium-sized family business. As an engineering company it is likely to be involved in manufacturing, and could well be function-based (Production, Purchasing, Accounts, etc.). As a `medium-sized´ company, it will probably have some form of hierarchy and chain of command. Since it is a `family´ business, it has probably grown from being a small business: the family are still in control, but the company´s culture and their management style isn´t clear. One of the first tasks the designers have is to analyse the company´s structure, culture and management style ✔ ✔, because how the company is run will influence the design of the MIS. For example, different managers at different levels will require different amounts and types of information (e.g. `strategic´ and `tactical´ information) ✔ ✔.

Related to this will be any proposed changes in organisation and structure, which the designers will have to take account of ✔. The crucial area for them is the nature of the information in the company: its sources, how it `flows´ through the hierarchy, how it is collected, stored, organised and transmitted ✔ ✔.

Questions with model answers

A grade candidate continued

For help see A2 Study Guide sections 4.1 & 4.2

The designers will also concentrate on the people currently employed: in particular, their existing computer skills and their feelings about a computer-based information system ✔. The final influence here will be the cost of the system. The company isn't a large plc, its funds may well be limited, and this could limit the extent of the MIS ✔ ✔.

Examiner's Commentary

This is a thorough and well-explained analysis of the case study information.

(c) It is clear from the question that the present level of information (quantity and quality) is not sufficient for the managers. If a computerised MIS is introduced, managers will gain as follows.

Communication should be faster: e.g. the network will offer e-mail facilities ✔ ✔. Information will be able to be manipulated more easily: examples include the use of spreadsheets, possibly for budgeting or forecasting, or calculating ratios, and databases for the various customers and suppliers ✔. This information will support the credit control system (e.g. by identifying and analysing `aged debtors´), and again improve communication, e.g. by using the computer system to generate paperwork such as invoices ✔. The company could also use dedicated software such as an accounting package to support this ✔. Since the company is in engineering, managers may use other specialist software, e.g. CAD/CAM (computer-aided design and manufacture). From a marketing point of view, perhaps the company could get a presence on the Internet, to promote itself ✔: access to the Internet will also help it obtain much more information (e.g. about competitors, or government statistics) ✔.

A good answer which selects key issues of not working and the use of computers, and applies them.

Overall, therefore, the company's data should be turned into meaningful information more easily, more quickly and more efficiently.

The problems the company may face include having to train managers and other employees in the use of this computer-based system ✔. Many people are still uncomfortable with using computers, and there would also be a cost factor in having to take people away from their jobs for training ✔. Second, computer hardware and software can date very quickly, so there is another cost-based issue, that of having to keep this system up-to-date (extra training would then be required, again costly) ✔. Finally, the company will probably have to meet the requirements of the 1998 Data Protection Act in terms of registration and disclosure of information, which adds to the administration required ✔.

Overall, however, it seems that the advantages of such a MIS outweigh the disadvantages, especially since the cost of the system is likely to be exceeded by the benefits accruing from it.

One of the strengths of this answer is in how it relates the MIS to the company, for example, by considering its different functions.

Exam practice questions

 *Answers on p. 68*

(1) R H Multimedia plc operates in a highly competitive and fast-changing environment. It employs 240 workers and has plants at three different locations. The firm is organised on a hierarchical structure with little worker participation. This probably arose as the firm has grown organically and is still largely owned and run by its founders.

However, changes are just around the corner. R H Multimedia plc has decided to introduce a flatter organisational structure with fewer levels of management and more employee empowerment.

(a) Suggest reasons for any business having to make changes. **[8]**

(b) Discuss:
   (i) the reasons why there may be resistance to change amongst the employees of R H Multimedia plc, and **[4]**

   (ii) ways in which management could minimise this resistance. **[6]**

(c) Evaluate R H Multimedia's decision to introduce a flatter organisational structure with fewer levels of management and more employee empowerment. **[12]**

[CCEA 2000 paper 1]

Answers

(1) (a)
- The business needs to stay competitive, and may have to improve its competitive position. It needs to react to competitors' moves, such as the introduction of a new competing model.
- There may also be technological advances that the business needs to incorporate into its work: if it fails to do so, its cost structure is likely to be less efficient than that of the competition.
- The business also needs to respond to changes in demand for its products: consumers' tastes change, and there are continuing demographic changes that may also affect the level of demand.
- Government legislation and other regulation changes, forcing the firm to review and if necessary change its practices (e.g. on employing people declaring a disability, on storing electronic data about customers, etc.).

(b) (i)
- This may be due to the attitude 'things are fine as they are', or there may be other reasons such as the fear of job losses or inability to cope with the proposed change.
- Evidence of 'little worker participation' suggests the management has probably not consulted staff about proposed changes: the fact that the company is based in three locations adds to the difficulty of communicating with employees.
- This lack of communication is an important factor as to why change may be resented.

(ii)
- A full and immediate involvement with the policy of change is important. Staff will be less resistant to change as a result of knowing what is going on and why, and how they will be affected.
- It also helps them recognise the need for change, and to accept that in the longer term – e.g. job prospects through the firm surviving and growing – change is beneficial.
- The change should be introduced gradually, and linked with appropriate staff training, and unions/employee organisations should be consulted.

(c)
- RH Multimedia operates in 'a highly competitive and fast changing environment'.
- With the pace of change, and the need to respond rapidly to this change, the company must be structured in such a way as to meet this challenge.
- Flatter structures are associated with swifter decision-making, and with quicker response to customer needs and requirements.
- Employee empowerment usually increases motivation, since staff are more involved in decisions and more responsible for their own actions.
- It is also often associated with greater financial incentives, better career paths, and greater promotional opportunities.

- A drawback associated with flatter structures is the increased spans of control.
- This may mean that a manager finds it difficult to exert proper control.
- Changes in job structure and operation can also cause conflict, and not everyone welcomes greater empowerment.
- If changes demotivate some staff, this could increase absenteeism and labour turnover.
- Overall, the decision should benefit the company and its employees, through allowing it to respond more quickly and effectively to changes in its environment.

Questions with model answers

C grade candidate – mark scored 15/30

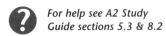

For help see A2 Study
Guide sections 5.3 & 8.2

Examiner's Commentary

Gillette has launched its new razor – the Mach 3. This is the company's biggest and most important new product for eight years, but will it be successful? Gillette has 71% of the North American and European market for razors and blades but investors have begun to worry about slowing growth, partly due to a smaller rival recently launching a new razor of its own.

Eight years ago Gillette was losing its grip on the razor market to cheap throwaways and facing yet another hostile take-over bid. Its new product at that time, the Sensor razor, saved the firm and today it is vastly stronger, being one of America's 30 biggest companies. The company also owns such brand names as Duracell batteries and Parker pens.

The Mach 3 razor will test Gillette's unusual approach to innovation in the consumer products business. Most companies produce in response to competition or demand but Gillette boasts that it launches a new product only when it has made a genuine technical advance. An example is the Duracell Ultra battery which is designed to last 50% longer than its rivals and is specially designed for palmtop computers and personal CD players which need and use a great deal of power. It is also priced at 20% more than a conventional battery. Gillette spends 2.2% of its turnover on research and development: that is twice as much as the average consumer products company.

Three-quarters of the money spent on the Mach 3 razor has gone on 200 new pieces of specialist machinery, designed in-house, which will churn out 600 new razor blade cartridges per minute, tripling the current speed of production. This means that the investment will pay for itself within two years. The fact that the company spends more on new production equipment than on new products is one reason why Gillette regularly hits its target of reducing manufacturing costs by 4% per year.

Another difference between Gillette and most other consumer product companies is that it does not tailor its products to local tastes. This gives it vast economies of scale in manufacturing. Gillette's products obviously have global appeal. Last year 70% of its sales were outside America. More than 1.2 billion people now use at least one of its products every day. The company has 91% of the market for blades in Latin America and 69% in India.

© *The Economist*, London, 18 April, 1998

(a) Explain the phases of development through which the firm's new Mach 3 razor is likely to have been taken. **[6]**

(b) Discuss the factors that Gillette may have considered when designing its new razor. **[10]**

Questions with model answers

C grade candidate continued

For help see A2 Study
Guide sections 5.3 & 8.2

(c) Evaluate the impact on Gillette of spending so much of its turnover on research and development that is not in direct response to competition or demand. **[14]**

[CCEA Specimen paper A2 1]

(a) The phases start with collecting and sifting through new ideas ✔. Once this is done, the firm starts looking at the likely success of the product. It will test-market it ✔ to gauge consumer reaction. If all goes well, the product will be launched ✔.

(b) The designers will need to consider the razor's costs when designing it: the razor can't be too expensive, otherwise the company will not make a profit on it ✔ ✔. How it is going to be made will also influence design: it must be capable of being made efficiently and easily, so the finished product is workable ✔ ✔. Lastly, the razor should be designed with a USP (unique selling point) in mind if at all possible, to differentiate it from all the other razors on sale ✔.

(c) Research and development is not guaranteed to give a company a return, but there is plenty of evidence that Gillette is doing well from its own research and development ✔. Gillette is obviously very successful, judging by its market share in its various markets. This is partly due to research and development leading to new technology, and better production processes – e.g. the specialist machinery can triple the current speed of production ✔ ✔. It has also helped Gillette produce other products that show a technological advance, e.g. the Duracell battery ✔ ✔. In doing so, Gillette can stay ahead of the market, and lead rather than follow ✔. Financially, we can offset the 4% savings in manufacturing costs against the 2.2% cost of research and development, which shows it is well worthwhile for Gillette to invest in this research and to develop new products ✔.

Examiner's Commentary

The phases between evaluating the idea and test-marketing the product have been omitted, and there is no application of this knowledge to the Mach 3 razor.

Terms such as 'workable' are rather vague, and should be clarified. Although this answer relates to the given product, it lacks the organisation and structure of the A grade one.

Even given the strength of evidence that R&D is benefiting Gillette, the candidate should still have presented evidence of the negative impacts of R&D expenditure.

A grade candidate – mark scored 29/30

(a) The normal stages of new product development, which apply to the Mach 3, include the following. First, new ideas for razors are obtained and then evaluated, to ensure good ideas are not rejected ✔. A prototype razor is then created and tested, to check likely market reaction (e.g. demand level) ✔ as well as the expected cost to see if it is financially viable ✔. The razor's design is then finalised, the razor developed, and test-marketed ✔. This takes place to assess whether the razor's target market (adult males) will react favourably to it ✔. The razor is then officially launched ✔, and starts its `life' in terms of the product life-cycle.

The stages are not just listed: there is also some description and explanation where required, all in the context of the Mach 3 razor.

Questions with model answers

A grade candidate continued

 For help see A2 Study Guide sections 5.3 & 8.2

Examiner's Commentary

(b) When designing a razor, Gillette's design team must have paid careful attention to safety requirements. Since Gillette exports its razors to many countries, it will need to be aware of safety regulations not only in the USA, but in its other markets (e.g. the EU countries) ✔ ✔. Related to this are consumer expectations of reliability: the razor will need to be reliable in order to be safe and to encourage repeat purchases ✔ ✔. The design team will also have wanted to design a razor that is pleasing to the eye (e.g. suitable use of colour in materials), but, even more importantly, one that is functional ✔ ✔. To be 'functional', a razor must be comfortable to handle and easy to use.

Effective linking of theory to this practical situation.

The design team will work closely with three business functions in particular. First, production: the razor should be easy to produce, making use if possible of existing equipment and staff skills ✔. Second, accounts: the razor must be capable of making a profit, so the design team will also have to bear in mind the financial implications of their design ✔. Finally, marketing: the marketing department will be looking for a design that helps the marketing of the new razor: issues such as display ✔ and storage ✔ will therefore be considered by the design team.

This is well-organised and analysed.

(c) There is plenty of evidence of a positive impact on Gillette as a result of its relatively high spending on research and development (R&D). The case study mentions that Gillette has 71% of the North American and European razor market, and substantial sections of other markets: the company will need to invest heavily in R&D due to the nature of its global market ✔ ✔. Gillette is a proactive company rather than a reactive one, because it seeks new technological development, and it also leads rather than having to respond to competitors' developments and initiatives ✔ ✔. The technology it gains from its R&D can probably be used to improve the production of its other products: the evidence is in reaching its target of a 4% cut each year in its manufacturing costs ✔ ✔. The investment in new technology resulting from R&D also has a quick payback period (a 2-year period is stated) ✔ ✔. Also, by developing 'in-house' Gillette becomes less reliant on outside suppliers, and is therefore in greater control of its own destiny ✔ ✔.

The candidate also uses production and financial terms and ideas effectively.

The risk remains that such a heavy expenditure on R&D may result in the company producing a product that isn't demanded ✔. There is also evidence that investment in R&D may not always yield the right answers or the right technology ✔ (e.g. when Gillette was hit badly by the development of competitors' cheap, throwaway razors) ✔. Overall, however, Gillette seems to be profiting from this major investment.

This answer draws effectively on the evidence presented in the case study.

Exam practice questions

 *Answers on p. 73*

(1) **(a)** Explain the importance of market research in the development of a marketing strategy for a new product. **[8]**

(b) Discuss how the marketing strategy of a soap manufacturer might differ from that of a car manufacturer. **[12]**

[WJEC Specimen paper BS4]

Answers

(1) (a) • 'Market research' involves obtaining primary and/or secondary data about the market for a product: e.g. consumer lifestyles, ages, buying habits, etc.

• 'Marketing strategy' refers to a business plan that will enable the firm to meets its stated marketing objectives.

• The strategy will consider elements of marketing such as the marketing mix, the product portfolio and its analysis, as well as the results of using techniques such as SWOT analysis.

• In developing a marketing strategy there will be a need to identify customers' needs in the market or segment that is being targeted, the nature and degree of competition, market trends, pricing patterns, and so on.

• Some of this information can be obtained through market research, which may be quantitative and/or qualitative in nature: for example, buyer behaviour could be determined through surveys or observation, and competitor policies and performance through statistical analysis. This evidence will contribute towards developing a medium- to long-term strategy.

Examiner's tip

A general explanation is acceptable, but remember to concentrate upon the role of market research in the context of new products.

(b) There are differences and similarities between the markets for soap and for cars.

• Both are 'mass' markets, both are at home and abroad, although different cultures, tastes and regulations (e.g. right-hand or left-hand drive; the acceptance of scented soaps) mean that these markets need researching carefully by both manufacturers.

• Although cars are thought of more as a 'luxury' and soap as a 'necessity', there are different segments in both markets (e.g. small hatchback/'second car' market compared with performance car market; everyday toilet soaps compared with luxury 'gift' soaps).

• As a result, both manufacturers' strategies will need to consider the relevant segment(s) in which the firm will sell, develop or enter, as well as the differing needs of consumers.

The soap and car markets differ in terms of the degree and type of competition.

• Both car and soap markets currently feature few producers who are often selling relatively similar products, so non-price promotion and competition are likely to be important features of the firms' strategies.

• The strategy for both manufacturers will probably try to identify some USP feature of their products, which is likely to be easier for the car manufacturer.

• Both strategies will probably feature persuasive and informative advertising, concentrating on the 'youthful' appeal of soap or some style/image feature for cars.

Examiner's tip

Remember to apply theoretical issues to the particular examples of soap and cars.

Questions with model answers

C grade candidate – mark scored 12/25

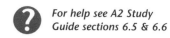

*For help see A2 Study
Guide sections 6.5 & 6.6*

Turner & Turner Limited makes lawn mowers. Most of the work is concerned with producing large grass cutters on which the operator can ride. Three models are made and the company also has a repairs and spares department. The engines are brought in from an overseas manufacturer and fitted to the mower that the company makes itself.

The company presently uses a full costing method but there are plans to cease production of the least profitable model. The following criteria will be used to allocate the overheads:

- Rent and rates will be allocated according to the number of machines sold;
- Power costs will be allocated according to the cost of direct labour;
- Administration costs will be split equally between the three models.

The selling price of each model and direct costs of production are shown below:

	Model A £	Model B £	Model C £
Selling price	2000	2800	3600
Direct materials	400	500	600
Direct labour	800	1000	1400
Engine	600	700	900
Units sold/year	80	120	200

The figures below show the overhead costs faced by the company.

	£000
Rent & rates	128
Power	16
Administration	39

(a) Using the proposed absorption costing method, calculate the total profits generated by each of the three models for the business. **[6]**

(b) Using the information available, calculate the contribution from each model. **[3]**

(c) Assess the consequences of the plan to cease production of the least profitable model. **[8]**

(d) The firm has been approached to supply 50 Model C machines to an overseas buyer. What advice on pricing the order would you give the firm? **[8]**

[Edexcel 2000 Paper 2]

Examiner's Commentary

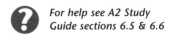

For help see A2 Study
Guide sections 6.5 & 6.6

C grade candidate continued

Examiner's Commentary

(a) Model:

	A (£)	B (£)	C (£)	
Unit sales revenue	2 000	2 800	3 600	
Unit direct costs	1 800	2 200	2 900	
Unit contribution	200	600	700	
Number sold	80	120	200	
Total contribution	16 000	72 000	140 000	✔✔✔
Less overheads:				
rent & rates	25 600	38 400	64 000	
power	4 000	5 000	7 000	
administration	13 000	13 000	13 000	✔
Profits	(26 600)	15 600	56 000	✔

(b) Contribution is shown in (a) as

A = £16 000, B = £72 000, C = £140 000 ✔ ✔ ✔

(c) Model A is obviously the product making the biggest (the only) loss, so dropping it would save the company a lot of money ✔. It loses £26 600 a year, so Turner & Turner will make a profit of £71 600, the profits for models B and C, if it is dropped.

(d) Turner & Turner Ltd can sell its model C at a price of £3 600 ✔. It will make extra profit, because all its costs have been paid by its current sales ✔ ✔. Selling 200 of model C makes a profit of £56 000, so an additional 50 will add another £14 000 profit.

> This display shows contribution, because here the direct costs are variable and the overheads are fixed costs. The candidate has not apportioned the power costs correctly, wrongly using the unit direct labour figures rather than the total figures.

> The candidate doesn't realise that fixed costs will still have to be paid regardless of whether the company makes three, two or even no models. The profits for B and C can't simply be added together if A is dropped from the product range.

> The candidate has made one relevant point, but the calculation of the additional profit is wrong: it isn't as simple as this!

A grade candidate – mark scored 25/25

(a)

	A (£ 000)	B (£ 000)	C (£ 000)	
Revenue	160	336	720	
Direct costs:				
direct materials	32	60	120	
direct labour	64	120	280	
engines 48	84	180		
Overheads:				
rent & rates	25.6	38.4	64	
power 2.206	4.137	9.655		
administration	13	13	13	
Total costs	184.806	319.537	666.655	✔✔✔
Profits	(24.806)	16.463	53.345	✔✔✔

Questions with model answers

A grade candidate continued

 For help see A2 Study Guide sections 6.5 & 6.6

Examiner's Commentary

Calculations:

rent & rates = A $\dfrac{80 \times £128}{400}$ B $\dfrac{120 \times £128}{400}$ C $\dfrac{200 \times £128}{400}$

power: A £64 000 + B £120 000 + C 280 000 = £464 000 total direct labour

power = A $\dfrac{64 \times £16}{464}$ B $\dfrac{120 \times £16}{464}$ C $\dfrac{280 \times £16}{464}$

> There are a lot of calculations for 6 marks, so make sure a suitable layout is used such as the one chosen here. Calculations are shown, which is important.

(b) The contribution from each model is:

	A (£)	B (£)	C (£)
Sales revenue	2 000	2 800	3 600
Direct (variable) costs	1 800	2 200	2 900
Unit contribution	200	600	700
Number sold	80	120	200
Total contribution	16 000	72 000	140 000 ✔✔✔

> Both unit and total contribution figures are shown. The tabular layout is both clear and time-saving, very important in an examination.

(c) The least profitable model is A, because using the absorption costing method it makes a loss of £24 806 ✔ ✔. It does, however, make a positive contribution to the fixed costs of £200 a unit, £16 000 on present sales ✔. In this sense it is `profitable´, and the question should be asked: is the apportionment of the (fixed cost) overheads fair? ✔ For example, it seems unlikely that model A will take a third of the administration costs, because it only makes up 20% of sales volume (80 out of 400) ✔. The apportionment of rent and rates on numbers sold can also be queried ✔. Turner & Turner Ltd must also consider the opportunity cost of dropping A. If it is dropped, this may allow competitors to enter the market ✔. Also, if A is dropped, can the company use the resources released more efficiently and profitably? ✔

(d) Assuming the company has spare capacity, it can afford to sell the 50 model C products at any figure above £2 900, which is the marginal cost for this model (the total direct costs) ✔ ✔. It can afford to do this because, at present sales levels, all fixed costs are covered by the contributions made by the three models ✔ ✔. Therefore, any additional items sold will bring profit as long as their selling price is above their variable cost - in this case, £2 900. The problem could be for Turner and Turner that, if it allows a `special low-price deal´, other customers may discover this and demand similar deals ✔ ✔. If the company thinks this won´t happen and it has spare productive capacity, it can decide on any price above the £2 900 figure. If it decides to sell at £3 600, it will make £700 profit ✔ on each item sold (£35 000 in total) ✔.

> The candidate is well aware of the marginal costing arguments here. The points are well explained, and supported by relevant figures and calculations.

Exam practice questions

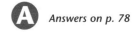

Answers on p. 78

Oakbank Foods plc is one of Europe's leading manufacturers of convenience foods such as ready meals, pizza, cakes and desserts and sandwiches. It manufactures its products in the UK, Holland, Republic of Ireland, Germany and Portugal and employs over 11 000 people. The company has a clear objective of being European market leader in a range of convenience foods.

The following is an extract from the company's operational review for 1999.

'In the Republic of Ireland and on the Continent the transition to Euro trading has gone smoothly. However, the early weakness of the Euro has restrained any major growth in direct exports from the UK.'

Information taken from the company's accounts is shown below.

	1999 (millions)	1998 (millions)
Turnover	£788.9	£774.2
Cost of Sales	£633.4	£613.8
Gross Profit	£155.5	£160.4
Net Profit	£27.4	£48.1
Dividends Issued	£17.7	£16.9
Current Assets	£169.4	£203.2
Current Liabilities	£200.7	£167.0
Total Capital Employed	£228.8	£280.3

	1995	1996	1997	1998	1999
Gearing Ratio	85%	79%	51%	34%	42%
Dividend per share	6.7p	6.7p	6.9p	7.3p	7.6p
Earnings per share	9.4p	11.3p	11.9p	13.4p	13.7p

(a) Calculate, for 1998 and 1999, the following ratios for Oakbank Foods plc (give your answer correct to one decimal place):
  (i) return on capital employed;
  (ii) net profit percentage. **[6]**

(b) Explain the extract from the company's operational review for 1999. **[10]**

(c) On the basis of the information in the case study, discuss whether or not a potential investor might be wise to invest in shares in Oakbank Foods plc. **[14]**

[CCEA Specimen paper A2 1]

Answers

(a) (i)   1999 = (27.4 × 100) / 228.8 = 12.0%
1998 = (48.1 × 100) / 280.3 = 17.2%

(ii)   1999 = (27.4 × 100) / 788.9 = 3.5%
1998 = (48.1 × 100) / 774.2 = 6.2%

(b)   Reference to the Euro is to the single currency adopted in 12 EU countries (excluding the UK): 'transition to Euro trading has gone smoothly' refers to the use of the euro as a trading currency.
- Oakbank Foods, having factories in Holland, Ireland, Germany and Portugal, can use the Euro in its inter-country trading. It will not be concerned with exchange rate fluctuations, but will face greater price transparency.

Reference to 'early weakness of the Euro' refers to its trading value against other currencies, notably the pound and dollar: in the first two years of its existence, the Euro fell against these currencies.
- This affects Oakbank because exports measured in sterling will be relatively expensive, and imports relatively inexpensive.
- As a result, UK exports are affected ('restrained any major growth in direct exports from the UK').

(c)   Arguments in favour of investing:
- increased turnover;
- higher dividends (over the five years dividend per share increased from 6.7p to 7.6p);
- earnings per share have also increased (9.4p to 13.7p).

Arguments against investing:
- reduced profitability – (a) shows falling net profit margin and return on capital employed;
- net profit margin has fallen by more (2.7%) than gross profit margin (from 20.7% to 19.7% = 1% fall), indicating expenses as a percentage of turnover have increased (from 14.5% to 16.2%);
- working capital ratio is now less than 1 (0.8) compared with 1.2 in 1998 – indicates worsening liquidity position;
- gearing has also increased since 1998, although it is significantly lower than five years ago.

Conclusion: there are some concerns about the company's present levels of profitability and liquidity. More information is required, which could be obtained from copies of the company's full final accounts.

Examiner's tip

Like many financial analysis questions, there isn't a simple answer. You need to concentrate on the key issues of profitability and liquidity.

Questions with model answers

C grade candidate – mark scored 10/20

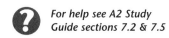

For help see A2 Study Guide sections 7.2 & 7.5

Bradley and Moores plc operates throughout the UK, making and assembling office furniture. Its plant in Birmingham is the largest of nine production centres. The main changes that have taken place recently are linked to the spread of information technology and delayering. Last year, the whole company was reorganised to meet the requirements of ISO 9001. Not everyone was happy with these changes.

Chelsea Rimmer, the firm's legal adviser, was about to have a meeting with the Assistant Personnel Manager, Hugh Hurley. Hugh began by explaining that there had been a dismissal in the Marketing Department. 'One of the account managers, Mark, who has had some sort of viral infection for years was dismissed by the Marketing Manager. It was felt that Mark had been using his illness as an excuse for having excessive time off. Eventually we just could not cope with his repeated absences. The work was not getting done.'

Hugh also outlined a second problem: 'I have just been made aware by our Production Manager of an incident that happened last week with one of the company's long-serving maintenance workers, Bob Malone. Someone tripped over some tools he had left out whilst he had a coffee break and broke his arm. I have spoken to Bob before about his untidiness, but it's not really my job to monitor him; that should be done by his line manager.'

After listening carefully to these two stories, Chelsea looked concerned. 'I should have been made aware of these problems earlier. I have been worried about the number of accidents happening in this company for some time now.'

(a)   Suggest what possible action may be taken by Hugh Hurley to reduce the number of accidents at the plant.   **[10]**

(b)   Discuss how these two cases demonstrate the existence of communication problems at Bradley and Moores.   **[10]**

(a) Accidents occur because there is not enough attention being paid to safe working. All companies must follow Health & Safety procedures and this company needs to follow the guidelines more closely. It may be better training that is needed ✔. *Workers may be unaware of the procedures to be followed, although we are told that Bob is a long-serving worker and so he should know better. Maybe he is not motivated enough. This can be improved by better pay or better conditions* ✔.

It may be that the managers are too busy to monitor all of the employees ✔. *We are told that the company has just gone through many changes for ISO 9001 and delayering* ✔. *This may have led to greater demands on the management so that they have neglected some of their duties* ✔. *It may be a good idea for the company to appoint a member of the company responsible for all safety issues* ✔

Examiner's Commentary

Although this answer does well to highlight possible causes of the accidents, very little attention is made to solving them, which is what the question is primarily about.

Questions with model answers

C grade candidate continued

For help see A2 Study Guide sections 7.2 & 7.5

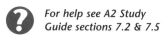

Examiner's Commentary

(b) The Marketing Manager should not be dismissing a worker. He does not know the correct procedure and may be accused of unfair dismissal. Full consultation should take place between the Marketing Department, Personnel Department and the legal adviser, before any decision is taken ✔. The fact that this has not happened shows a lack of communication and suggests that this normally happens which is quite worrying ✔. There is little point employing a legal adviser and then not making full use of her. Did he know about her presence? Did he know that he should confer with the Personnel Department? ✔

The actions of one person may have serious repercussions for the firm in the future. If clear communication systems had been in place this would not have happened ✔.

If a question refers to two cases and you only talk about one, then do not be surprised to score less than half marks, however good your answer is.

A grade candidate – mark scored 19/20

(a) The first thing that Hugh should do is to gain more information about the accidents that have taken place, what department they occur in and how they happen. He should be looking for any patterns that may identify the reason for the accidents occurring ✔. It may be that the accidents are mostly occurring in one department. It may also be the case that although accidents are occurring in different departments, their causes may be similar. Is it a lack of training, poor communication, poor management or a general lack of care amongst the workforce? ✔

A good start to the answer. A problem cannot be solved until the causes are known.

It is the managers of each department who are ultimately responsible for everything that happens within their department. Hugh will need to ensure that the managers are fully aware of the health and safety issues that are relevant ✔. It is highly likely that there is much machinery and dangerous equipment involved in the production of office furniture ✔. It may be that the obvious dangers are well protected. From the evidence about Bob, however, it may be that the more minor dangers are being ignored ✔.

This answer avoids the mistake of repeating legal facts. It is the application of law that is most important.

Once the causes of the accidents have been identified, Hugh will need to ensure that all managers and workers are clear about their own responsibilities. If necessary, better induction and training should be provided. There will be a cost involved; however, this cost must be weighed against the loss of earnings from regular accidents, never mind the potential bad publicity ✔.

This is the first step towards providing an evaluative answer.

The cause of the accidents may be less obvious. The time taken recently to gain ISO 9001 certification may have distracted everyone from other issues, and the fact that not everyone was happy with the changes may lead to a lack of motivation. Both of these factors may have meant that health and safety issues have been given a low priority recently. A look at the accident figures for the last few years will make interesting reading ✔.

Questions with model answers

A grade candidate continued

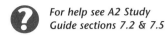

For help see A2 Study Guide sections 7.2 & 7.5

Once Hugh has identified all of these issues, he will have to establish an action plan or strategy to begin the task of minimising accidents in the future. Initially this may involve increased training and monitoring of workers ✔. Those such as Bob may have to be formally reprimanded, which may eventually lead to dismissal, so that the message of safe working is taken seriously by all. A culture of safety in the workforce will require changes amongst managers and workers to reverse the recent trends ✔.

Good answers to this sort of question require a clearly thought-out strategy, as covered here.

(b) Circumstances surrounding both cases highlight serious communication problems at Bradley & Moores. The accident happened last week, but the Personnel Department have only just been made aware of it. Although you would not expect every single accident to be reported immediately to the Personnel Department, one as serious as this, where an employee will be missing from work, is something that will have an impact on the firm ✔. Either the system of reporting accidents is inefficient so that the message does not get through quickly enough, or even worse, there is no clear system for communicating such matters ✔. Information about accidents does not appear to be widely known. If Chelsea Rimmer, who is `only´ a legal adviser, is aware of the problem then so should the management in the company ✔.

The ability to suggest more than one cause will encourage analysis and evaluation in an answer.

The lack of action by Bob´s Line Manager shows poor communication, either because he did not know about the problem, or because he has failed to ensure that Bob did not improve ✔.

The Marketing Manager has dismissed a member of staff without consulting the Personnel Department. This is very worrying as the Personnel Department is ultimately responsibly for the hiring and firing of all employees ✔. The Marketing Manager may not have authority to dismiss workers, which may lead to claims of wrongful dismissal. He may be unaware of the legal issues involved, which may cost the company a lot of money in the future ✔.

All of the above communication problems may be the result of the recent delayering exercise carried out by the firm ✔. Although the eventual result of this process should be to improve the efficiency of communication ✔, it may be that in the immediate term it has caused problems. This may be because managers and employees are not yet used to their new responsibilities or communication channels ✔. Although we would expect things to improve with time this may not be before the problems created have had serious repercussions throughout the firm. For this reason it is imperative that the company approaches the correction of these communication problems with the highest priority ✔.

A good holistic view of the problem that gains top marks.

Exam practice questions

Answers on p. 84

BROMSBRIDGE COLLEGE

Wasim Ahmed had joined Bromsbridge College to take up his post as Human Resource Manager in July 1999. He had previously worked as Assistant Personnel Manager for a well-known chocolate manufacturer. Bromsbridge College, although one of the country's smaller colleges, offered him promotion, and new challenges.

He had been appointed to the Senior Management Team of the College to replace Bob Pickard, who had resigned after a series of disagreements with the Principal, Duncan Holt. The other members of the team are the Finance Manager, the Curriculum Director, two Curriculum Managers, and four Team leaders for four faculties.

During the final week of Bob Pickard's notice period, Wasim had taken the opportunity to acquaint himself with some of the issues that Bob had been dealing with recently, and to try to get a feel for the way that Human Resource issues in a Further Education College might differ from those in a major manufacturing company.

Bob Pickard had been extremely forthcoming about some of the personalities and issues with which Wasim would be faced. Bob had also provided Wasim with some interesting data which he had gathered (See Table 1 and Table 2).

'If you want my honest opinion, you could write down all you know about Human Resource issues and people skills on the back of a postage stamp, and still have room to spare. Duncan Holt came here five years ago with big ideas about cost cutting and efficiency movements. He pretends to consult with staff, but in truth he is usually only telling them what he wants to do.'

Bob had also explained that many of the longer serving members of the teaching staff had taken early retirement between 1994 and 1998. Whilst this had saved considerably on the salary bill for teaching staff, it had removed many of the experienced and highly motivated staff. Where necessary they had been replaced by part-time lecturers, and also younger, more recently qualified lecturers.

Bob also told Wasim that teaching staff were having to teach larger classes, and were also expected to make return journeys of up to 20 miles to teach at any of the College's four sites. As a result staff seemed to complain much more about the expectations that were placed upon them by their team leaders and the Senior Management Team.

Bob had continued by telling Wasim that relations with the Lecturers' Union were at an all-time low, and that a lot of his time had been taken up with negotiations concerning the introduction of teacher appraisal, and negotiations relating to the replacement of all part-time teaching staff with lecturers supplied by an employment agency specialising in supplying teaching staff. The Union members are getting really angry because they can see that Duncan Holt intends to get his own way, and even the newer members of staff are becoming more angry about the current state of affairs.

Wasim was not at all surprised to be called to the Principal's office the day after Bob Pickard left. Duncan Holt informed him that his two key tasks in the immediate future were to:

1. Have a strategy in place to implement teacher appraisal by January 2000.

2. Make the necessary arrangements for part-time lecturing staff to be replaced by agency staff by January 2000.

He informed Wasim that he was used to having his orders obeyed, and told Wasim that these deadlines were not hopeful guidelines – they must be achieved or else.

Wasim began to study the information given to him by Bob Pickard to see if there were any particular clues which might help with the tasks set for him by Duncan Holt. Perhaps life at the chocolate factory hadn't been all that bad really!

Table 1: Staffing Levels:

Year:	Management:	Teaching staff: Full-time:	Part-time:	Full Time Equivalent	Admin & Support
1993/94	16	94	29	(5)	26
1997/98	10	52	44	(8)	38
1998/99	10	50	48	(9)	52

Table 2: Teaching staff – Days lost through illness:

Year:	Full-time:	Part-time:	Most reported illness: (days lost)
1993/94	277	32	Colds and Flu
1997/98	792	49	Stress

(a) Discuss the problems that Wasim might face in his working relationship with Duncan Holt, the College Principal, given Duncan Holt's apparent management style. **[12]**

(b) Wasim has been informed that one of his key tasks will be to introduce teacher appraisal by January 2000. Suggest a strategy which Wasim might recommend in order for the scheme to gain the acceptance of full-time teaching staff. **[15]**

[OCR Specimen Paper – Further People in Organisations (Question 1)]

Examiner's tip

These questions make up just less than half of a module paper. They should therefore be completed in less than 45 minutes.

Answers

(a)
- Duncan appears very autocratic. Will Wasim be able to produce new ideas based on HRM theory in this atmosphere?
- Duncan is very clear about what he wants. How might Wasim react to his suggestions being rejected? Is this what led to Bob Pickard leaving?
- Will Wasim's lack of knowledge of educational establishments put him at a disadvantage when dealing with Duncan?
- Will Wasim encounter problems because of the attitude of the staff?
- How will Wasim's own motivation be affected by Duncan's style and demands?
- Will Wasim be allowed to freely make his own plans?
- Will Wasim be seen as a 'servant' of the Principal, to carry out his wishes regardless of the workforce's opinions? Will the staff co-operate with Wasim's proposals?

Examiner's tip

How Wasim might overcome some of these problems will need to be explored to gain a top mark.

(b)
- Wasim will need to prioritise the elements of his strategy carefully.
- He will need to consult with the teaching staff, their Unions and possibly ACAS.
- There is some evidence that the staff are going to be resistant to change. They will be unlikely to co-operate in the current climate.
- Wasim will need to investigate the best way to introduce appraisal. It will be very different for him as there are less obvious measurements of output than you would find in a chocolate factory.
- Wasim will also have to ensure that any strategy he produces is acceptable to Duncan Holt. What is acceptable to Duncan may be very different from what is acceptable to the staff.
- Will the process be rushed? We are told that there have been many changes in the staff recently and their workload has been increasing.
- How will the part-time staff and agency staff being introduced be appraised?

Examiner's tip

When a question asks for a strategy you must not produce an answer of unconnected points. You need to bring the different ideas together, preferably with a time-scale to show how the scheme may be introduced.

Questions with model answers

C grade candidate – mark scored 10/20

 For help see A2 Study Guide section 8.1

Hollinshead Fabrics Ltd is a fast-expanding family firm that produces children's toys made from pieces of material that are stitched together by hand into animal shapes. The Operations Director, Imogen Hollinshead, has just learnt that an order placed by a large toy store has been returned because most of the stitching on the toys is fraying. She is concerned as this is the fourth order returned, from different retailers, this month. Imogen feels that it may be time to replace the traditional method of quality control at the end of the production line.

(a) Explain two possible costs of poor quality control for Hollinshead Fabrics Ltd. **[6]**

(b) Assess possible quality control methods that Imogen could put in place. **[8]**

(c) Analyse how Hollinshead Fabrics Ltd may gain from internal economies of scale. **[6]**

(a) Two possible costs are the materials that have to be scrapped ✔ *and the costs of lost orders* ✔. *Because products are faulty they will have to be thrown away and this will cost a lot of money. This means that the company will make less profit* ✔. *Also, because of poor quality, the company will find it difficult to get more orders from this company and other toy shops. They will have to spend more money on advertising to regain the confidence of consumers.*

(b) Imogen should increase the amount of quality control taking place. More people checking the work being done will help to identify the workers who are not good enough ✔. *These workers can then be replaced or retrained.*

They may also want to increase the amount of machinery used ✔. *This will reduce the potential for human error, and so improve the reliability of output. Perhaps she should consider introducing the use of Computer Assisted Manufacturing (CAM)* ✔, *where the workers only have to push buttons on a machine to make sure that it does not go wrong.*

(c) The company may gain purchasing economies of scale. This is because they may now be able to buy in bulk, which is usually cheaper per unit ✔. *They will also find it cheaper and easier to borrow money, as banks will be happier to lend money to larger firms* ✔, *since they are less risky* ✔. *Marketing economies may also be gained* ✔.

Examiner's Commentary

If you compare this answer to the A grade answer that gains full marks, you will see the main difference is the use of the information given about Hollinshead Fabrics in the question. If you do not make sure that your answer is specifically about the company you are given information about, it is very unlikely that you will get more than half marks for the question. Although there are some well-explained points, the answer lacks detail, and some of it is not related fully to the question asked.

This is a poor answer, because no attempt has been made to look at the implications of the suggestions made; for example, could a family firm afford to buy the CAM technology? There is also very little use of the case material.

Although this student's answer shows evidence of knowledge, it does not contain any context. The key word in the question is analyse. This requires detailed discussion of links, implications and, if necessary, criticisms.

Questions with model answers

A grade candidate – mark scored 19/20

 For help see A2 Study Guide section 8.1

(a) One cost of poor quality control is the effect on the company's reputation ✔. Any adverse publicity that may occur will be particularly bad for a small company such as Hollinshead Fabrics, as they will rely on 'word of mouth' to create orders from other firms ✔. If a potential customer finds out about these returned products they may be reluctant to order from this company themselves ✔.

A second cost will be that of reworking the returned products to bring them up to the standard required to make them saleable ✔. Not only will the costs and hence profits be decreased, there is the potential knock-on effect of delays to other orders ✔. Because the toys are handmade the workers will have to spend a great deal of time concentrating on the returned products, rather than producing new products ✔.

(b) One possible system could be to introduce random checks, at all stages of the production line ✔. However, the fact that the current system of quality control is not working may suggest that this system of a third party checking the work of others is not working ✔. An alternative would be to introduce a system of Quality Assurance, maybe as part of a Total Quality Management strategy ✔. It may be that the material is received from the supplier in a poor state. If quality control takes place at the end of the production line, this fault will not be noticed until a lot of work has taken place ✔. Far better for this material to be identified as not being up to standard at an early stage ✔.

If each worker is given responsibility for quality, this will not only increase the amount of quality checking taking place ✔, but it will also make the workers feel more involved in the company, so increasing their motivation and sense of commitment to the company ✔.

(c) Economies of scale arise when an increase in output leads to a fall in average costs. Internal economies are those that only benefit the individual firm ✔.

Hollinshead Fabrics may benefit from cheaper raw materials, because as they grow in size they will be able to buy in bulk, which usually reduces the unit cost ✔. Financial economies may also be present. As the firm grows they will be able to negotiate cheaper rates when borrowing money and, because of their increased assets which act as security, they will be able to borrow more money ✔.

However, they may find it difficult to benefit from technological economies of scale ✔. As firms grow they are usually able to invest in more advanced and efficient technology ✔. Given the highly labour-intensive nature of the fabric toys, it may not be possible to carry out the production by machine ✔.

Examiner's Commentary

Recognition that being a small cmpany will cause specific problems is good context.

With 6 marks on offer for two costs, it is clear that the greater detail found in this answer is necessary.

As is expected in the A2 papers, this candidate has taken a strategic approach, examining the implications for the policies being suggested.

A clear definition of a difficult concept.

Excellent use of context.

Exam practice questions

A *Answers on p. 88*

A building project consists of a number of distinct activities (A to I) as shown in the table and network diagram below.

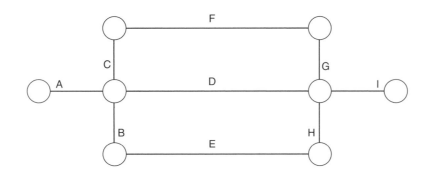

Activity	Duration in days
A	1
B	3
C	5
D	2
E	3
F	4
G	4
H	2
I	2

(a) (i) What is the earliest starting date for each of activities C, H and I? **[3]**

(ii) What is the latest finishing time for each of the activities D, E and H? **[3]**

(b) Identify and calculate the duration of the critical path for this network. **[3]**

(c) (i) Explain what is meant by the term total float. **[2]**

(ii) Calculate the float times that exist on each activity. **[3]**

[Edexcel Specimen Paper Unit 4 – Question 2 (a–c)]

Answers

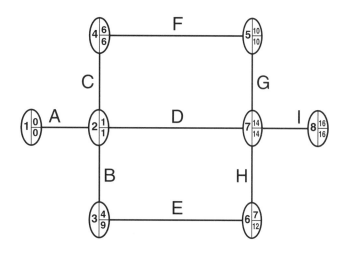

(a) (i)   C = 1, H = 7, I = 14

(ii)   D = 14, E = 12, H = 14

(b)   The Critical Path is A, C, F, G, I. It takes 16 days.

(c) (i)   The total float is the amount of time an activity can be delayed without it affecting the total length of the project.

(ii)   A = 0, B = 5, C = 0, D = 11, E = 5, F = 0, G = 0, H = 5, I = 0

Mock Exam 1

1 hour 15 minutes

Read the following extract and then answer the questions which are based upon it.

FORD MOVES EUROPEAN HQ OUT OF BRITAIN

Ford has moved the headquarters of its European operations from Britain to Germany. The shift is intended to increase the American group's competitiveness in the continent's biggest single market, Germany. The move will be seen as a blow to the prestige of British industry. Ford of Europe has been based in Warley, Essex, not far from Ford's Dagenham plant, since Henry Ford II, grandson of the company's founder, set up the European organisation in 1967. Ford of Europe are now based at Cologne, Germany.

The shift may arouse fears about Ford's commitment to Britain. Its Welsh engine factory in Bridgend is at present competing with German and Spanish plants to win a project for which Ford are seeking about £60 million in aid from the British government. There have also been intermittent concerns about whether Ford would maintain its dual site engineering operation in Europe, under which design and engineering is divided between Cologne and Essex. However, the company has invested heavily in its Essex facility in recent years. As evidence that there is no intention of pulling back further, Ford can point to its decision to expand the production line at Dagenham, the lead plant in Europe for production of its Fiesta car. In addition, Ford's newly created Premier Auto Group, which is made up of Jaguar, Aston Martin, Volvo and Lincoln, is based in Britain.

Ford of Britain has also been the test-bed for Ford's efforts to establish itself as the world's leading supplier of automotive services as well as vehicles. In April, Ford surprised the European car industry when it paid £1 billion for Kwik-Fit, the vehicle-repair chain. It is also expanding into car retailing and financial services in Britain. Ford has successfully resisted challenges to its position of market supremacy and it has more than an 18% share of the UK car market. But Ford is struggling in Germany where its market share, excluding Jaguar, has slipped below 9% this year. As a result, its European share has skidded well below the 12% at which it stood two years ago.

Ford managers believe that only by rooting itself in Germany can Ford of Europe avoid being handicapped in its attempts to match its American arch rival, General Motors, and the European market leader, Volkswagen. Success in Germany is crucial to Ford's attempts to improve sluggish profitability. Germany is almost twice the size of the next-largest European markets – Italy, Britain and France – and accounts for about one quarter of total west European car sales. General Motors has established a European lead over Ford thanks largely to its presence in Germany where its Opel brand is seen as German, whereas Ford is seen as a foreign brand.

Source: adapted from *The Sunday Times*, 22 August, 1999

Answer both questions. The questions relate to the article but your answers should not necessarily be limited to the material in it.

Question 1

(a) Ford is a company principally involved in motor vehicle manufacture and as such might be regarded as a secondary sector business.

    (i) Giving an example of each, identify the other two sectors of economic activity.

               [4]

    (ii) Discuss to what extent Ford can be regarded as a secondary sector business. **[10]**

(b) Discuss the major environmental influences affecting the way in which Ford operates. **[15]**

Question 2

(a) The article suggests one reason why Ford has moved its European HQ to Germany is '... to improve sluggish profitability'.

    (i) Outline two other possible objectives Ford may have been pursuing when deciding to move its European HQ to Germany. **[4]**

    (ii) By considering the determinants of demand, discuss why the German market is 'almost twice the size of Britain's'. **[10]**

(b) Discuss the objectives the British government may have in giving Ford financial aid for its Welsh engine plant. **[15]**

Source: OCR Unit 1
Specimen Paper

Mock Exam 2

1 hour 15 minutes

Answer all questions

Question 1

Willy Wonka is the secretive confectionery entrepreneur in Roald Dahl's children's classic *Charlie and the Chocolate Factory* who refuses to let outsiders on to the premises because of his paranoia about spies. The real chocolate barons were a lot more eccentric.

Forrest Mars, the now retired patriarch of Mars Inc. is one of the most private and successful entrepreneurs in the world. He remains one of the most mysterious figures in the history of corporate America. The man built a £6 billion a year confectionery empire. He adopts an **autocratic leadership style**.

Joel Glenn Brenner, who revealed the findings of an eight-year investigation, uncovered a world where industrial spies trade in secret recipes and inside information and where paranoid executives are locked in mortal struggle for market share.

Mars senior (Frank) began selling confectionery in 1902 at the age of 19 in Tacona in Washington State. In 1923, the Milky Way bar, which was known outside America as the Mars bar, was introduced and quickly established itself. This was followed by the Snickers bar, originally named as Marathon in Britain.

In 1932, Forrest Mars, Frank's son, left America for Britain. He took with him the recipe for the Mars bar and established the factory in Slough. The bar was made entirely by hand and proved to be so popular that Mars had to double his staff in six months.

Today Mars products are sold in more than 150 countries. The company is run jointly by John Mars and his older brother Forrest Junior. The Mars family wealth is estimated at $10 billion.

Mars has a reputation for treating its employees well; it is a **single status company** where management and employees work under the same conditions. Nobody has a secretary, everyone makes his own photocopies and takes his own phone calls. John Mars is probably the only chief executive officer of one of America's most powerful companies who still clocks in like a factory worker. Cleanliness is an obsession. The company's boast is that at any given time the level of bacteria on a Mars factory floor is less than the average level in a household sink. Quality is a compulsion. A pinhole in a Snickers is reason enough to destroy an entire batch.

Source: adapted from *The Times*, 11 February, 1999

(a) Explain, with the aid of an example, the meaning of 'autocratic leadership style'. **[4]**

(b) Analyse the reasons why Mars chooses to operate as a single status company. **[8]**

(c) Quality is a major objective of Mars. Discuss how human resource planning might help them to achieve this objective. **[8]**

Question 2

Study the information below and then answer the questions that follow.

It's never been tougher for suppliers in the United Kingdom motor industry. The market is global and fierce as suppliers strive to meet manufacturers' demands for high quality parts at the lowest cost, often in competition with cheap imports. Today's car buyers have high expectations. They look for value for money, expecting their new car to live up to the claims made, and have no hesitation in shouting loudly if it does not. Correspondingly, the car manufacturers expect suppliers to turn out parts to high specification and at the lowest possible cost. They demand that suppliers fit into their **JIT production schedule**. To satisfy these demands and to keep ahead of cheap foreign imports, suppliers must ensure the best quality at the right time.

To increase profits they need to be constantly finding more cost-effective and efficient ways of working. As markets become global, firms find it increasingly difficult to compete with low-wage economies. One technique used is **benchmarking**. Benchmarking has proved to be a useful tool for many businesses. One of its major contributions has been to encourage businesses to recognise that they can do better. Once a problem is recognised it is easier to find a solution.

Source: adapted from articles in *Business Review,* November 1998

(a) What is meant by the phrase 'JIT production schedule' as it applies to the motor industry?   **[4]**

(b) Outline the technique of benchmarking and analyse, with the aid of examples, how this can help the United Kingdom motor industry.   **[8]**

(c) Discuss ways in which suppliers to the United Kingdom motor industry can become more cost effective and efficient.   **[8]**

Source: WJEC Unit 3
Specimen Paper

Mock Exam 3

1 hour 15 minutes

Question 1

Read the extract and answer **all** parts of the question which follows.

BIG MAC BLUNDER HITS McDONALD'S

McDonald's is planning to push ahead with a range of other sales promotions to mark its 25th anniversary in the UK despite this week's Big Mac fiasco.

However, the burger giant is unlikely to repeat the 'Buy One Big Mac, Get One Free' offer which it launched in December to cover Christmas 1998 and the New Year. This promotion led to one of the biggest marketing errors in UK history.

McDonald's ran into problems last weekend with some restaurants experiencing eight times the usual demand for Big Macs, which sell for £1.99. The 'Two for One' offer meant that there was effectively a 50% price cut. Several restaurants were forced to close due to overcrowding and many customers were turned away when Big Macs ran out.

Television advertising was used to promote the offer, but a large number of restaurants found they could not cope. The Independent Television Commission will consider 21 complaints from the public. McDonald's was rapped by the tabloid press, labelled as 'Ham Bunglers' and 'Silly Burgers'.

The burger chain took full page advertisements in national and regional papers to apologise for the confusion.

Source: adapted from Ian Darby, *The Guardian*, 7 January, 1999

(a) Why do you think McDonald's used television as a means of advertising this sales promotion? **[5]**

(b) Examine the likely marketing objectives behind the promotions used to celebrate the 25th anniversary of McDonald's in the UK. **[6]**

(c) Calculate the price elasticity of demand for Big Macs if, as a result of the 'Two for One' offer, total sales increased from 2 million to 4 million Big Macs. **[5]**

(d)   Explain why McDonald's often uses psychological pricing for many of its products, such as charging £1.99 or £2.95.   **[4]**

(e)   To what extent might the 'Buy One Big Mac, Get One Free' marketing disaster have been a result of poor market research?   **[10]**

Question 2

Read the extract and answer **all** parts of the question which follows.

SCUNPOOL UNITED

Scunpool United Football Club is a small club playing in the lower reaches of the Third Division of the Football League. The club is not a profitable business and gate money is falling as spectators prefer to stay at home and watch the Premier League on television.

The club's accountant has drawn up a cash flow forecast for the season ahead.

All of the following forecast figures of cash inflows and outflows are based on last season.

The club plays twenty matches at home per season and expects an average crowd of 3 000, with each spectator paying £8 per match. The club also expects to reach the second round of two cup competitions and to receive a total of £50 000 gate money from these matches.

Other receipts come from a club lottery and anticipated income for the season is £50 000.

Additional income, estimated at £90 000 for the season, is derived from selling advertising around the ground and in match-day programmes.

Expenditure on match days is budgeted at £5 000 per match and for cup matches there has to be extra policing, increasing the budgeted total cup expenditure to a total of £30 000.

The biggest costs to the club, however, are the players' wages which are based on a 17-man squad earning an average of £25 000 per season. Other staff wages per season amount to £80 000. The manager, Kevin Smith, earns £50 000 per season.

The ground needs urgent maintenance to meet the local council's Health and Safety standards and £80 000 has to be set aside for this before the season starts.

Other overheads include insurance, heating and telephone bills. This additional expenditure adds up to £20 000 over the season.

Variable costs include the production of the match-day programmes and certain ground staff who are paid on match days only. The club has an overdraft limit of £500 000 and the current overdraft is £200 000. The great hope is that one of the younger players will be snapped up by All Star United, a Premier League team.

(a) Explain what is meant by the terms:

  (i) 'overheads' (line 23) **[2]**

  (ii) 'variable costs' (line 25) **[2]**

(b) Complete the cash flow forecast (attached) for Scunpool United's next season. **[9]**

(c) Scunpool United is not a profitable business. Examine the circumstances in which any business can survive without profits. **[8]**

(d) Evaluate ways in which Scunpool United could improve its cash flow. **[9]**

ATTACHMENT TO ASSESSMENT UNIT

Cash Flow Forecast for Scunpool United Football Club

Cash In:	£
Gate money	
Cup revenue	50 000
Club lottery	50 000
Advertisements and programme sales	90 000
Total cash inflow	

Cash Out:	
Match day expenditure	
Policing	30 000
Wages	425 000
Other staff	80 000
Manager	50 000
Ground maintenance	80 000
Other	20 000
Total cash outflow	
Net Cash Flow	
Opening Bank Balance	
Closing Bank Balance	

Source: AQA Unit 1
Specimen Paper

Answers

(1) (a) (i) Primary Sector – e.g. Fishing or Oil exploration.
Tertiary or Service Sector – e.g. Car servicing or Hairdressing.

(ii) A secondary sector business is one that is involved in manufacturing. The production of cars clearly involves the making of goods. However, Ford own Kwik-Fit which is involved in repairing and servicing cars, which is in the tertiary sector. There is also mention of car retailing and financial services, which although related to cars is not manufacturing.

Examiner's tip

Using the evidence from the case material to back up your arguments about non-manufacturing aspects within Ford will help you achieve a score above half marks. To score top marks you will need to evaluate which aspects of their business are the most important to Ford, which will ultimately determine whether they are correct to assume they are a secondary sector business or not.

(b)
- Social – smaller families will lead to smaller cars.
- Legal – changes in the speed limit may affect the production of faster cars.
- Economic – increased disposable income means that cars are no longer seen as a luxury.
- Environmental – increased awareness by society of health and pollution issues will influence research into cleaner cars.
- Political – fewer tax incentives for company cars or road tolls will affect demand.
- Technological – greater use of automation/robotics will affect costs of production.

Examiner's tip

This type of question produces the most waffle from students. Focus your answer on issues that specifically affect a car producer such as Ford. One example from each section above is still probably too many. How the change will impact on Ford and what they may have to do in response is what the examiner wants to read about.

(2) (a) (i) Possible objectives include increasing the market share in Germany, stopping the decline in market share in Europe or improving the image of the company compared to its main rival GM.

Examiner's tip

The key word in the question is 'Outline'. Only a very brief comment on each objective is required.

(ii) The main determinants of demand can be split into two categories, price and non-price (population, income, and taste).

Price may be cheaper in Germany, something we hear about constantly at the moment. It may also be that the price German consumers pay is less because of lower VAT or car tax, as well as the long-run costs of running a car, e.g. petrol prices, road tax, repair cost.

Non-price factors may include the following:

- Germany has a larger population and may buy a larger proportion of new cars compared to second-hand cars.
- Do Germans have a higher standard of living, which allows them to buy more cars and renew them more often?
- The Government may provide tax incentives for German consumers to buy more environmentally friendly cars.

Examiner's tip

The suggestions made are possible explanations. You are not expected to know about the German economy in any detail, but should be able to integrate the knowledge of business with a general knowledge of recent EU issues.

(b) Possible objectives include:

- To keep Ford in the UK to protect and create jobs directly and indirectly.
- To minimise the effect on the Government's Budget through loss of income tax and increase benefits if the Ford workers in the UK lose their jobs.
- Loss of jobs in such a deprived area as SE Wales will have a larger effect on the region's economy.
- Engines would have to be imported in the future which would affect the UK's trade balance.
- The loss of engine production may be the first step of a gradual withdrawal of all of Ford's UK operations.

Examiner's tip

You need to produce a balanced discussion of the objectives mentioned and the desired outcome.

Answers

(1) (a) The keeping of decisions at the top of the management hierarchy, usually because it is felt that staff are not able to make correct decisions or a decision has to be made quickly. For example, if the Mars company wanted to launch a new chocolate bar the decision would be made without any reference to middle and junior managers.

Examiner's tip

The question asks for an example, so it is very important to include one.

(b) Possible reasons include:
- To minimise the possibility of a 'them and us' attitude between management and workers.
- To improve staff morale.
- To show greater respect for individuals, which ties in with the theories of Mayo and Herzberg.
- To show that all employees are working for the same purpose with shared goals.

Examiner's tip

The phrase 'single status company' is not one that you will have definitely encountered in your studies. However, by reading the last paragraph of the article carefully it is clear what the phrase means.

Examiner's tip

The key word is 'analyse' so no attempt at evaluation is required.

(c) Possible ways in which workforce planning aids quality include:
- Helps in setting clear goals that are communicated to the workforce.
- Ensures tight supervision and discipline.
- The right workers can be recruited.
- Appropriate induction and training can be provided in preparation for future needs.
- A good appraisal system can be put in place to act as a monitor of standards and provide suitable motivational rewards.
- A fair level and method of payment can be put in place.

Examiner's tip

The basic knowledge outlined needs to be applied specifically to Mars and linked with how quality is therefore improved.

(2) (a) Suggested definition: A system of carefully planned scheduling to minimise the costs of holding stocks of raw materials, work-in-progress and finished goods. A car manufacturer would not hold large stocks of windscreens, which take up space and may be damaged while waiting to be used.

(b) Benchmarking involves identifying businesses that are accepted as being the best at a particular activity. Different companies may be used for different activities. By using this technique, a company is able to identify those aspects of production that can be improved and may act as a motivator.

The UK motor industry may benefit from this in a number of ways:
- It is a quicker way of rectifying a problem. Given that the UK lags behind its major competitors it will be able to incorporate ideas that they can see are already working, rather than starting from scratch.
- UK car firms will be more aware of their relative performance.
- Car buyers' expectations are more easily satisfied if the UK company is striving to achieve the same standards as their European competition.

Examiner's tip

There is a need to link these points with the evidence in the question for top marks.

(c) Ways in which suppliers can become more cost effective and efficient:
- Better staff training to help them see their important role in the supply chain.
- Change production methods to flow, to even out the supply levels.
- Increased use of technology.
- Increased size of operation to benefit from economies of scale.

Examiner's tip

Good answers will recognise that changes in the production method or increased technology will be expensive and disruptive, ultimately with the potential for costs to exceed the benefits hoped for.

Answers

(1) (a) Possible reasons include:
- They could afford it.
- The ability to reach a mass audience.
- By choosing when to show the advert relevant target segments can be reached.

2 marks for reasons and up to 3 marks for developing the reasons in relation to the context about McDonald's.

(b) Likely marketing objectives include:
- Increase sales revenue.
- Increase market share.
- Raise awareness or image of the business.

Examiner's tip

'Examine' requires you to assess the possible objectives and briefly consider how successful the promotions used would be in achieving these objectives.

(c) Price Elasticity of Demand = $\frac{\text{Percentage change in demand}}{\text{Percentage change in price}}$

$$= \frac{100\%}{50\%} = 2$$

(d) Psychological pricing can include the practice of setting a price below the barriers, perceived by consumers, at £2.00 or £3.00, etc. This may be because:
- Competitors do it.
- Market research has suggested that this price is most acceptable to customers.
- Buyers believe that they are getting a good price.

(e) Poor market research may have meant that:
- Marketing planning was carried out based on poor forecasting.
- There was a lack of understanding between the amount of promotion and the likely response in demand.
- There was no consideration of the staffing and production limitations. However, in defence of McDonald's, it is difficult to make forecasts especially around Christmas and New Year and, as not all restaurants were affected, it was not a complete disaster. There is also the old saying that there is no such thing as bad publicity. McDonald's certainly got more free publicity out of the events.

(2) (a) (i) Suggested definition: Costs that are not directly attributable to one particular aspect of production, for example, rent, heating & lighting.

Examiner's tip

Overheads are not the same as fixed costs. Overheads can be fixed (e.g. rent) or variable (e.g. advertising).

(ii) Suggested definition: Costs that vary in direct proportion to output, for example, match day programmes.

Examiner's tip

3,000 spectators paying £8 each for 20 matches a season.

(b) Gate money = 3 000 × £8 × 20 = £480 000

Therefore Total cash inflow = £480 000 + £50 000 + £50 000 + £90 000
= £670 000

Match day expenditure = £5 000 × 20 = £100 000

Therefore Total cash outflow
= £685 000 + £100 000 = £785 000

Examiner's tip

The entries on the attached cash flow forecast show 6 separate cash-out entries totalling £685 000.

Examiner's tip

A bracket signifies a negative figure.

Net Cash Flow = £670 000 – £785 000 = £(115 000)

Examiner's tip

This is the current overdraft.

Opening Bank Balance = £(200 000)

Closing Bank Balance = £(200,000) + £(115 000) = £(315 000)

Examiner's tip

Any mistakes made in the early part of the question will lead to a different answer. however, you will still be given up to 8 out of 9 marks for a wrong final answer, so long as the examiner can clearly see the method you have used.

(c)   It is possible to survive without profits because:
- In the short run cash is more important than profit.
- The overdraft will allow survival in the near future.
- In some businesses, especially football, investors may have other motives than profit and are willing to inject their own capital without any need for financial returns.
- The company may have built up reserves during previous more successful years. However, in the long run profits are vital in most businesses to ensure survival.

Examiner's tip

The overriding issues here are the objectives of the business. If the football club is just a hobby of a wealthy individual then the usual business concerns are less important.

(d)   The club could:
- Sell star players.
- Reduce the size of its playing squad.
- Reduce its other staffing and general running costs.
- Look for extra sponsorship.
- Increase match day prices.

Examiner's tip

The likelihood of success and the impact on the club of these suggestions are vital for top marks. Would selling players not lead to worsening performances on the pitch so that attendances, and hence revenue, will fall?

Mock Exam 1

1 hour 30 minutes

Read the case study and answer **all** the questions which follow.

THE TAKE-OVER

Arthur James studied the figures carefully. As the Chief Executive of ATCO plc he had been the driving force behind the recent take-over of Chiltern Products plc, and was determined to ensure that it proceeded smoothly. The offer price for the Chiltern Products' shares had valued the company at £55 million, compared to the balance sheet value of £45 million. This has angered some of ATCO's institutional investors who felt that the bid overvalued Chiltern Products' intangible assets.

ATCO's Marketing Director, Basil Tapanayagar, disagreed with this view. 'Chiltern Products plc has an excellent reputation for lounge and dining-room furniture, and its brand names will be a tremendous acquisition for ATCO. Furthermore, unlike our own company, it has integrated vertically by moving into furniture retailing, with 10 stores in London and the South East.'

Basil recognised, however, the limitations of Chiltern Products' range of products, in contrast to ATCO's broad product portfolio of both domestic and office furniture.

Integration of the marketing of the two ranges was considered to be a major challenge to the newly formed, integrated company, which would trade under the name of 'Fine Furnishings plc'. It had been agreed to use both the ATCO and Chiltern Products brand names, as the two brands appealed to very different market segments, but ATCO management would be responsible for the marketing of both brands.

ATCO had employed the 'marketing model' as a means of guaranteeing clear planning and monitoring of its marketing activities. However, Chiltern Products' marketing had been disorganised, with no overall direction being provided. As a result, many of its product ranges were in direct competition with each other. Basil considered his main priority to be the development of a clear marketing strategy for the Chiltern Products division.

In the industry, 'Chiltern Products' was recognised for the excellence of its staff and the high quality of its products. These factors had enabled it to continue to flourish during both booms and recessions. The 'task culture' of the organisation was based on small groups of employees working on individual projects with considerable autonomy. These projects had enabled talented staff to utilise their skills, without the limitations imposed in companies with more traditional hierarchical structures. These teams had created a number of successful new products.

The restructuring of the company had been the major obstacle in the negotiations leading to ATCO's offer finally being accepted. ATCO was organised in a more traditional way, based on a 'role culture' and with clearly defined lines of responsibility and authority. The span of control was low and there were many levels of hierarchy. Decision-making was methodical but slow, and this had caused frustration amongst many of the junior and trainee managers. There was a 35% rate of labour turnover amongst these staff, well above the rate experienced with other employees.

ATCO's progress had been mixed during the last decade. During the boom of the 1980s it had benefited from the growth in home ownership, with particular successes in its targeting of cheap bedroom and dining-room furniture. The recession and then the relatively high value of the pound had led to a decline in market share in the early and mid-1990s. The company responded by modifying its South Wales factory, despite opposition from local residents who were concerned about the location of the factory on a rural site. This now operated as an assembly line for imported components, allowing the company to benefit from cheaper imported materials whilst avoiding the high transport costs incurred by rival companies whose products were manufactured abroad. However, high wage costs combined with low productivity in the factory meant that losses had been recorded for some years. A new training scheme was introduced in order to improve the quality and flexibility of the workforce.

In contrast, ATCO's more exclusive ranges of lounge furniture and office equipment, produced in High Wycombe and Nottingham respectively, sold well throughout this period. It was recognised that ATCO's ability to create high added value through the strength of its brands was good, but some of its investors questioned its reluctance to rationalise both its product range and labour force. In comparison to its main rivals, ATCO was considered to be a labour-intensive organisation, and its reluctance to invest in new production techniques was considered to be a weakness. Trade union influence was strong, with 95% of factory workers and 50% of white collar workers in a union. There was no trade union representation at Chiltern Products.

ATCO's decision to import materials initially encountered trade union opposition, but promises that there would be no redundancies had overcome these objections. It was now widely recognised that the decision to restructure the South Wales operation had saved 5 000 jobs in that area. ATCO also received praise from environmental groups for its policy of only using wood from renewable forests. In contrast, Chiltern Products had been criticised severely for its move away from UK suppliers towards the importation of non-renewable hardwoods from tropical rainforests. Pressure groups had also highlighted its recent policy of sub-contracting assembly work to low wage countries in order to reduce costs.

Table 1: Economic indicators

	Current year	Next year (forecast)
Unemployment (%)	6.50	5.00
Inflation (%)	2.30	2.70
Economic growth (% change)	1.50	3.20
Bank base interest rate (%)	6.25	7.00
Value of £ (in Euros)	1.42	1.35

(1) To what extent might the Chiltern Products division benefit from the introduction of more scientific decision-making through, for example, the adoption of the 'marketing model' (line 19)? **[14]**

(2) Evaluate the difficulties that Fine Furnishings plc might experience in attempting to unify the two distinct business cultures that currently exist. **[14]**

(3) How might a social audit help Fine Furnishings plc deal with the possibility of adverse comments from pressure groups? **[16]**

(4) Assess the likely impact on a furniture company of the forecast changes in the economic indicators shown in **Table 1.** **[18]**

(5) Provide a reasoned judgement on the merits of the take-over of Chiltern Products plc from the viewpoint of ATCO plc. **[18]**

Source: AQA Unit 6
Specimen Paper

Mock Exam 2

1 hour 45 minutes

Study the information provided in the case study entitled Rentokil Initial PLC and answer the questions that follow.

RENTOKIL INITIAL PLC
COMPANY PROFILE

Although this company has made its name (in the eyes of the consumer) with either pest control or with appliances found in public lavatories, it provides a broad range of services to cater for diverse markets: healthcare, pest control, security services, contract cleaning, tropical plants (for company reception areas and offices), air conditioning systems and office machine maintenance. The company operates worldwide. Although growth in Europe has been static, the company has found new markets in the Far East; Malaysia, Thailand, Hong Kong and Indonesia have all provided the company with new markets that have grown quickly. All of these markets (despite the speed of growth) have been cash-generative.

The company provides useful evidence as to why there has been a growth in service industries over the past 15 years. With an overall RONA (return on net assets) of 99%, this provides excellent opportunities for good bottom-line results (i.e. after-tax profits). A service industry will not have a large investment in fixed capital; Rentokil's only major investment is in portable machinery and in vehicles. The company's stock levels are (by definition of a service company) very low and therefore it operates with a low level of working capital and keeps a control of cash flow in this respect.

Rentokil sells a product that the consumer demands and it is capable of charging premium prices (margin = 23.8%); with a high margin and an efficient use of assets, the RONA result is easy to appreciate. 'Sales per employee' is low compared with other companies, mainly because it is a labour-intensive business which relies on contact with the customer through a service (which uses people) rather than a product (which uses capital).

Source: adapted from the Internet

RENTOKIL'S TAKE-OVER OF BET

For the past ten years Rentokil Initial has been one of the success stories of British industry. The company's chief executive Sir Clive Thompson has shown how it is possible to make money from some quite unlikely projects where other services companies have had far less success. The rewards to shareholders have been excellent.

On 29 April last year Rentokil Initial bought a large British company, BET, for £2.1 billion. For many years BET has been badly underperforming with profit margins of 7% compared to an industry average of 14%. Sir Clive has announced that he intends to keep those parts of BET where he believes that 'we can improve performance in the medium term and add value'; the remainder of BET's concerns and any of Rentokil Initial's that are not performing well will be sold off to the highest bidder. Likely companies for sell-off include Rentokil Initial's timber preservatives business and BET's US resorts and UK plant-hire operations.

Rentokil Initial's success has been built on a strategy of targeting the middle and upper end of the market – customers who appreciate a superior service and are prepared to pay for it. Against the odds they have created a premium brand in a rather unglamorous industry. Sir Clive intends to do the same thing with BET. He has promised to double margins at BET within two to three years. 'We will change the customer mix, shifting it from the bottom- and mid-end of the market, to the upper end, which pays more.' Some progress has already been made on cutting costs by the closure of three of BET's offices. The following three years will see efforts focused on improving sales and marketing.

Source: adapted from an article in *The Independent on Sunday*, 19 January, 1997 and Rentokil Initial's internet home page

RENTOKIL INITIAL PLC: KEY DATA 1993–97

(a) Rentokil's turnover and profits 1993–1997
(b) Segmental analysis of Rentokil's turnover and profits

(a) Rentokil's turnover & profit 1993–1997

Year to 31 March	1993	1994	1995	1996*	1997*
Turnover (£bn)	0.6	0.73	0.86	2.45	3.43
Pre-tax profits (£m)	147	177	214.5	335	475

*forecasts

(b) Segmental analysis of Rentokil's turnover & profits

Turnover (£m)	6 months to 30 June, 1996	6 months to 30 June, 1995	Year to 31 Dec, 1995
United Kingdom	343.4	177.3	358.5
Continental Europe	194.4	92.4	195.6
North America	220.8	63.4	164.9
Asia, Pacific and Africa	83.4	67.8	141.1
Total	842.0	400.9	860.1
Environmental Services	313.1	286.5	594.7
Environmental Property Services	184.6	114.4	265.4
BET Services	344.3	–	–
Total	842.0	400.9	860.1
Profit before tax			
United Kingdom	56.4	42.0	91.3
Continental Europe	35.6	25.8	54.0
North America	16.6	8.0	18.7
Asia, Pacific and Africa	28.7	20.5	44.0
Total	137.3	96.3	208.0
Environmental Services	101.5	84.6	180.2
Environmental Property Services	14.1	11.7	27.8
BET Services	21.7	–	–
Total	137.3	96.3	208.0

A PROFILE OF SIR CLIVE THOMPSON, CHIEF EXECUTIVE OF RENTOKIL

Clive Thompson is a hands-on manager/control freak who cares a great deal about detail. During Rentokil's bid for BET he has led from the front. Clive is not the sort of chief executive who leaves drafting meetings to the advisers. He is very much in charge. Thompson likes to ask questions, to challenge, to set his own agenda, to argue the toss. Part of his management style is to create tension, to be unpredictable. A good talker, his marketing background and his experience as South East chairman of the Confederation of British Industry have taught him how to be aggressive without being nasty.

Despite his achievement in building Rentokil from a domestic £100m company in 1982 to an international business services group valued at £3.6m today, he has a surprisingly low profile for the head of Britain's 53rd largest company. 'Throughout my life I have tended not to conform', he says. 'I tend to be anti-establishment, radical and I like to have fun. I think being conformist is boring.'

Thompson could be accused of exploiting low-paid labour for shareholders' dividends. But he refuses to confuse his business goals with his social aims. '**When you are running a business the social and moral aims are secondary**. It is not my job to make people happy; it is my job to enhance shareholder value. But you can ensure shareholder value by ensuring people feel fulfilled in their jobs.'

Source: adapted from *The Sunday Telegraph,* 14 April, 1996

(1) Explain the benefits that Rentokil might hope to gain from the take-over of BET. **[8]**

(2) 'An effective marketing policy alone is not sufficient to guarantee success in a global market.' Discuss with reference to Rentokil. **[8]**

(3) Various stakeholder groups have an interest in the overall performance of Rentokil between 1993 and 1997. Assess the performance of Rentokil from the viewpoint of two stakeholder groups. **[10]**

(4) Discuss the factors in the internal and external environment that may cause Sir Clive Thompson to modify his management style at Rentokil. **[12]**

(5) Discuss the view expressed by Sir Clive Thompson in paragraph 3 above where he states: "When you are running a business the social and moral aims are secondary." **[12]**

Source: WJEC
Specimen Paper BS6

Answers

(1) At present, there is evidence that Chiltern Products has a relatively limited product range (para. 3), and disorganised marketing (para. 5). This suggests the lack of clear overall strategy/marketing objectives.

Adoption of the 'marketing model' will ensure that Chiltern Products examines how market-oriented it is, and analyses the effectiveness of its marketing mix. Its internal structure, quality of its products and staff (paras. 2 and 6) suggest it can complement ATCO, but clearly its product range needs careful review due to the existence of internal competition (para. 5).

Examiner's tip

Although the question uses the 'marketing model' as an example, note that its focus is broader than this, so your answer shouldn't be limited to marketing-specific issues only.

Introducing a more scientific decision-making model should ensure the Chiltern Products division focuses more clearly on medium- and long-term strategy, setting achievable and realistic objectives at all levels. The degree and effectiveness of how Chiltern Products' activities are presently controlled isn't clear from the case study, but its relatively unstructured and less traditional organisation (paras. 6 and 7) suggests a less rigorous set of controls than would be found under more scientific decision-making. The effectiveness of budgeting, sales forecasting, and HRM decisions should all improve as a result of using a management by objectives (and also management by exception) approach.

There is an indication that Chiltern Products has the potential to respond effectively to change: para. 6 indicates excellent staff, high-quality products, and an existing 'task culture'. There is some evidence of effective decision-making: para. 5 suggests that Chiltern Products is an effective innovator, and this asset/skill mustn't become submerged if a more scientific decision-making model is adopted.

Examiner's tip

You should always consider the relevance of 'change' in this type of question.

(2) Evidence is that ATCO has a role culture (para. 7), and Chiltern a task culture (para. 6). ATCO has gained some benefits from operating using a role culture (paras. 8 and 9), and Chiltern from its task-based operation (para. 6). Arthur James will recognise the value of the innovative, quality-driven approach that is the strength of Chiltern Products, which could be lost through imposing ATCO's role culture. He may also be reluctant to introduce the task culture throughout ATCO, whose culture currently provides clearly defined status and responsibilities.

Examiner's tip

Questions like this expect you to recognise that there is no easy answer, and that there are likely to be strengths and weaknesses associated with whatever you suggest. You need to ensure that your answer is sufficiently analytical, and doesn't simply describe the strengths and weaknesses of these different cultures.

In trying to create a unified culture, Arthur James faces these problems:

- Potential loss of the clearly defined hierarchical structure at ATCO;
- This may lower motivation at ATCO due to the loss of status for some staff;
- The likelihood of higher LTO at Chiltern's junior management level if the ATCO culture is adopted;
- The potential loss of Chiltern's innovative skills;
- Possible alienation of both groups of staff, particularly those of Chiltern Products;
- The general problem of adapting to, and coping with, change.

Examiner's tip

The easy way to structure your answer is to examine the issues from ATCO's perspective, then from Chiltern's, then general issues such as the dislike of change – extra marks can be gained from exploring the general effects of change on people and systems.

(3)   The pressure groups that appear to be particularly influential in this situation are:

(a) Institutional investors – concern over share and intangible asset valuation, adoption of suitable long-term strategic policy, lack of capital investment.

(b) Trade unions – how ATCO handles the take-over in terms of redundancies, redeployment, training and retraining opportunities, union representation of former Chiltern staff, pay policy, effects of future investment on jobs.

(c) Staff – similar issues to those for the unions, also adoption of an acceptable 'culture'.

(d) Environmental pressure groups – Chiltern's policy of using non-renewable rainforest sources.

(e) Local communities – location and employment issues.

Examiner's tip

With a question like this you need to examine carefully the case study content: in this situation there is a wide range of possible pressure groups that need to be identified, together with their likely concerns.

A social audit examines, in quantitative terms, how a firm's activities affect society: these activities include such things as health and safety, and pollution. The audit will produce evidence that can be used in relation to the concerns of these groups. Although the evidence may be more obviously associated with the concerns of particular groups only – e.g. environmentalists, rather than institutional investors – any resulting improvement in aspects such as public image can be used to counter adverse comments from any source.

Examiner's tip

You will have studied 'social audits', and it can be useful for you to show understanding of terms like this. Don't spend too long doing this, since the question expects you to analyse and evaluate, rather than just show knowledge.

A general benefit from social auditing is that it produces evidence that Fine Furnishing's directors can use to publicise the success of its social policies. Results of the audit can be used as a defensive ploy, providing evidence of action taken in response to criticism from any of these pressure groups. Fine Furnishings can also use results internally, e.g. to adapt its structure and culture in such a way as to recognise and take account of social issues more obviously.

Examiner's tip

The size of the change is worth commenting on: for example, there are substantial changes forecast in unemployment and economic growth, compared with a slight change in base rates.

(4)
- Unemployment forecast to fall. Fewer suitably qualified people in the labour market from whom to recruit; likely higher wage demands; but higher demand levels for furniture in the economy (more employed and therefore increased spending power).
- Inflation forecast to rise. This will increase raw material prices and lead to higher wage demands, but the increase is not substantial. Its effect will be particularly influenced by the value of the £ and level of economic growth.
- Economic growth forecast to rise. Substantial increase forecast, which will increase consumer spending power: this is likely to result in a more than proportionate increase in demand for products such as furniture.
- Bank base interest rate forecast to rise. This will increase lending costs: if Fine Furnishings is highly geared, this will be a major increase in its costs, affecting profitability. May cause a delay in the expected capital investment. Will also reduce consumer spending power, e.g. through mortgage rate rises, leading to greater reluctance to buy on credit, hitting demand for furniture and other high-priced items bought this way.
- Value of £ forecast to fall against the euro. Leads to greater price competitiveness within Europe. Effect on imports from outside the EU difficult to forecast.

Examiner's tip

You must consider the nature of Fine Furnishings plc – selling expensive/luxury items, overseas suppliers, comparatively labour-intensive – but you don't have to include a detailed evaluation of all five economic indicators to gain high marks. What is important is to show (a) that you understand the general significance of each indicator, and (b) how it is likely to influence the work of a furniture company such as Fine Furnishings.

(5)
ATCO should gain from the general benefits associated with both horizontal and vertical integration. Horizontal integration should bring greater (internal) economies of scale for ATCO, e.g. increased purchasing power, and greater market share/power with reduced competition (Chiltern now being part of ATCO). Vertical integration brings ATCO greater control over suppliers, and the guaranteed sales outlets offer closer contact with customers.

Examiner's tip

In approaching this question, structure your answer by considering both the 'general' and the 'particular'. When you explain the general benefits/arguments in favour of take-overs, make sure you relate these to ATCO and Chiltern.

Specifically, Chiltern has an 'excellent reputation' (para. 2), appeals to a different market segment (para. 4), employs talented staff and produces high-quality products (para. 6). It is also innovative, with a track record of successful new products (para. 6). As a result ATCO will diversify, and should benefit from Chiltern's reputation.

However, if Chiltern's intangible assets have been overvalued (para. 1), this could affect medium-term profitability as these asset values are written off against profits/reserves, possibly affecting investor confidence and Fine Furnishing's share and dividend performance. There is evidence that Chiltern offers only a limited product range (para. 3), with an inefficient marketing function (para. 5), a conflicting culture (para. 7) to that prevailing in ATCO, and a poor environmental record (para. 10). There is also no guarantee that Chiltern's existing outlets will be suitable for ATCO products.

Examiner's tip

There is a need to present a balanced argument: you're not asked for a detailed conclusion/recommendation because the take-over has occurred.

(1) BET also appears to be an international company, which will help Rentokil develop globally to an even greater extent. Rentokil will also diversify further: this spreads risk and helps ensure survival. Economies of scale should accrue to Rentokil, e.g. purchasing, marketing and financial.

Examiner's tip

The question specifically asks for 'benefits', so there is no need to construct a balanced 'for and against' type of answer here.

(2) There is evidence that Rentokil has an 'effective marketing policy': for example, it has diversified into different markets that are proving cash-generative, and its turnover/profit figures outside the UK increased substantially in the first six months of 1996 compared with 1995. Any company, including Rentokil, will have to cope with the problems associated with global markets: e.g. differences in culture and language, exchange rate fluctuations and restrictions on international trade, possible political instability in certain countries, and the need to recruit, retain and communicate with reliable staff and agents overseas. Although Rentokil appears to have a sound financial base (segmental analysis data), it will still face the above difficulties.

Examiner's tip

Your answer should relate to marketing policy for businesses based in a global market: you could therefore consider a range of marketing issues such as market research and new product development, in addition to the 'four Ps'. You could also support your assertions with calculations from the segmental analysis. Balance the answer by referring to both marketing difficulties – e.g. language and culture – and other non-marketing specific issues such as employment and legislation overseas.

It often pays to select two quite different stakeholders, which allows you to use a range of evidence. Selecting two stakeholders with similar interests, such as shareholders and managers, can lead to a lot of repetition in your answer.

(3) Shareholders: specifically interested in return on net assets (i.e. return on capital employed), total profits and whether the net profit margin is increasing, an assessment of liquidity to assess whether Rentokil can meet dividend payments, and share prices (which will be influenced by profitability and expansion).

Examiner's tip

You can support these points with segmental calculations, e.g. NP margins for each of the three segments, and reference to the growth in the share price.

Employees: also interested in profitability and share price information since the more successful the company, the safer their jobs appear to be and the more likely they are to negotiate a beneficial pay rise. Employees may also be part of a share/profit scheme, so they would have a direct increase in profits and share prices. They are also interested in expansion, since this increases numbers employed and possibly their promotion prospects.

Examiner's tip

A stakeholder often overlooked is the local community. Rentokil's local communities will be interested in factors such as how much tax the company is paying, and its local employment policies and financial support schemes. The difficulty of selecting the local community is that there is usually little numerical evidence on which you can draw, as is the case here.

(4)   Evidence suggests that Sir Clive Thompson has an autocratic, rather than a democratic, leadership/management style. The company's performance suggests this is not an inappropriate style to adopt at present, but as the company continues to grow he may find it more difficult to remain on top of detail and impose his own personality throughout the organisation. As a result, he may be forced to delegate and encourage a more democratic approach than that which currently exists. Also, if the takeover of BET or further expansion affects profitability/share price, he may be forced into adopting a different style. Other external factors such as the effect of legislation or regulation (e.g. European-style Works Councils), or the influence of pressure groups, could lead to changes in management style.

Examiner's tip

Regarding internal factors, you can base your answer on the likelihood that the company's internal structure and culture is continuing to evolve and change: although the leadership style can help mould these changes, it will also have to accommodate them to a certain extent. The main external factors are suggested in the given profile, i.e. the importance of maintaining growth and share/profit performance and how this interacts with the adopted style.

(5)   There is evidence that Rentokil accepts that social and moral aims are in some ways secondary: e.g. employment of low-paid labour, also the possible use of polluting chemicals, and the way it interacts with overseas environments such as those in 'developing countries' where multinational operations have sometimes been of a lower standard than their operations in more developed economies. His beliefs will have to be adapted to fit legal requirements, e.g. data protection legislation, regulation on the control of substances hazardous to health.

Examiner's tip

You would normally be expected to draw on a number of different business aspects: it's useful with such questions to consider social, legal, economic and political issues. In this question you can easily contrast social issues with legal/political ones.

There is also evidence that Sir Clive Thompson is aware of the value of social/moral aims: e.g. his reference to the importance of employee satisfaction, and how this can influence shareholder satisfaction. As a labour-intensive employer, Rentokil will be aware of the importance of motivated employees, and of meeting its employment obligations that relate to social contentment (e.g. meeting the minimum wage, operating in a safe way, encouraging staff involvement and providing opportunities, e.g. for promotion.)

Examiner's tip

Quite clearly, although the quote mentions these aims are 'secondary', the case study suggests Sir Clive Thompson clearly recognises the value of acceptable business social/moral behaviour, e.g. in the way that this affects shareholders' views of the company.